THE BRIDLEWAY

THE BRIDLEWAY

*How Horses Shaped the
British Landscape*

Tiffany Francis-Baker

BLOOMSBURY WILDLIFE
LONDON · OXFORD · NEW YORK · NEW DELHI · SYDNEY

For Olive and Dave, my sun and moon

BLOOMSBURY WILDLIFE
Bloomsbury Publishing Plc
50 Bedford Square, London, WC1B 3DP, UK
29 Earlsfort Terrace, Dublin 2, Ireland

BLOOMSBURY, BLOOMSBURY WILDLIFE and the Diana logo are
trademarks of Bloomsbury Publishing Plc

First published in the United Kingdom 2023

A catalogue record for this book is available from the British Library
Library of Congress Cataloguing-in-Publication data has been applied for

ISBN: HB: 978-1-3994-0318-4; Audio download: 978-1-3994-0627-7;
ePub: 978-1-3994-0320-7; ePDF: 978-1-3994-0319-1

2 4 6 8 10 9 7 5 3 1

Typeset in Bembo Std by Deanta Global Publishing Services, Chennai, India
Printed and bound in Great Britain by CPI Group (UK) Ltd., Croydon, CR0 4YY

MIX
Paper from
responsible sources
FSC® C020471
www.fsc.org

To find out more about our authors and books visit www.bloomsbury.com
and sign up for our newsletters

Contents

They shut the road through the woods
Seventy years ago.
Weather and rain have undone it again,
And now you would never know
There was once a road through the woods
Before they planted the trees.
It is underneath the coppice and heath,
And the thin anemones.
Only the keeper sees
That, where the ring-dove broods,
And the badgers roll at ease,
There was once a road through the woods.

Yet, if you enter the woods
Of a summer evening late,
When the night-air cools on the trout-ringed pools
Where the otter whistles his mate,
(They fear not men in the woods,
Because they see so few.)
You will hear the beat of a horse's feet,
And the swish of a skirt in the dew,
Steadily cantering through
The misty solitudes,
As though they perfectly knew
The old lost road through the woods.
But there is no road through the woods.

'The Way through the Woods', Rudyard Kipling

CHAPTER ONE

The Warren

The blackthorn flowers arrive before the leaves. All at once, born from the gloom of late winter, a froth of blossom pours from black bark tipped with poisoned thorns, new life pitched against death until the leaves emerge later and bridge the void. When the flowers bloom, they sing like sirens to the bumblebees, so round and velvety they make a *donk* against kitchen windows on their way to find food. All winter the queens sleep beneath the earth, waking only when they feel the sun warming the soil. First they seek their flowers for energy, then back they fly to search for holes and clumps of grass in which to make their nests.

One morning in late March, I heard a bumblebee hovering behind my head as I rode. Like the swifts that would scream their arrival a few weeks later, bees are more often heard before they're seen – their lazy, drunken murmur so distinct from the uptight vibrato of a wasp. I had paused beside a blackthorn tree and could feel the bee floating next to my ear before it passed so close to my cheek that I couldn't help recoiling, remembering when I once stood near an open beehive and three honeybees got caught in my hair. The bee flew down to Roxy's nose, but she didn't move, disinterested in something so small. Horses can spook at the strangest things – hose pipes, wheelbarrows, a road sign that's moved two inches from where it was before. All harmless, but perhaps there is something in their intuition that makes them fear humanmade objects and trust the wilder things of the world, even if they have a sharper sting.

The bee flew on, and I turned my gaze back to the Hangers. Roxy and I had been out riding for an hour through the holloways and wooded downs of east Hampshire, the March light bright but cool in the shade.

We had paused halfway along a quiet lane to drink in the view before descending into the chalk combe ahead. To my left stood a large country house; beyond it, the landscape rolled down and up again, a postcard-perfect vision of the South Downs.

The word 'hanger' comes from the Old English *hangra*, meaning a steep, wooded slope. In autumn, when the mists rise out of the beech trees, they seem to almost 'hang' from the hillside. Yew berries fall to the ground and redwings take shelter in the bare trees. And in spring, the sunlight filters through the treetops and turns the leaves lime green, the surrounding chalkland erupting with orchids and butterflies. The Hangers in late summer are beautiful, yet something stronger draws me to the earliest days of spring when the weather is still unreliable, but the first signs of life appear on the trees. It is like licking the spoon while the cake is still baking; a taste of what is yet to come, sweet, warm and full of hope.

I nudged Roxy into a slow walk, and we continued down the road, leaving the view behind and beginning our descent into the combe. A stocky, cob-like animal, I wasn't sure whether Roxy was classed as a horse or a pony. I've never been good at remembering how many hands a horse measures – a 'hand' being the official unit of height for a horse in the UK – but whether we class them as a horse or a pony tends to depend on their height. All I could determine of Roxy was that she was white with black patches – and quite round. As an ex-eventing horse, she was fast when she wanted to be and had plenty of stamina, but she didn't compete anymore and had podged out slightly. Having never been a competitive rider, I preferred hacking out into the woods and fields, so I had been borrowing Roxy from her owner to give us both some exercise. Secretly, I cherished her roundness. She was soft, sturdy and comfortable, the perfect companion with whom to bumble through the deep dells and bridleways of the South Downs.

Our path into the woods was festooned with wildflowers; celandines tangled up with violets and primroses, dog's mercury and white dead-nettles unfurling into the sun. But as we slipped beneath the canopy, a shadow crept over the path, and the brightness was extinguished, replaced instead with a bower of yew and beech branches clawing across the sky. The light levels were low here, particularly at the top of the slope before the coppiced ash and hazel trees at the valley bottom let the sun swim back in. It is so dark that this is one of only three places in Britain you can find a particularly rare helleborine orchid – one that thrives in shadow that I had tried many times to find without success.

Roxy and I moved further into the combe and I could smell the soil stirring, the dampness, the white slips of chalk suspended between roots that pushed deeper into the ground with every passing spring night. Not for the first time in my life, I felt like I was 'going to earth'. The writer Mary Webb used that term as the title of her 1917 novel about a woman caught between the natural world and the world of men. As a phrase, it means to retreat to a place of safety, coined by hunters to describe a fox that has escaped underground. These three words come to me from time to time as I drift through wild places like this, where the trees are old and the air swells with life and decay. When the 'civilised' world feels inhospitable, uncomfortable, there is something about going to earth, seeking out deep, green spaces, that feels like sanctuary – like going home.

The Warren is aptly named, a labyrinth hidden within a deep chalk combe known locally as Doscomb. Here, in the south-east of England, a combe is generally described as a short valley or hollow on the side of a hill, often wooded but with no river running through it. Today, the paths that zigzag through the Warren are kept clear by conservation groups, though, in the past, they would have been formed and shaped not only by walkers, riders and travellers but by every other creature that has crept through this place over the last few thousand years. In Oliver Rackham's *The History of the Countryside*, he points out how our idea of 'highways' – roads, bridleways (or bridle paths) and footpaths that simplify a traveller's journey to their destination – existed long before humankind started shaping them. Deer, badgers, foxes and otters all make paths to find food, water, shelter and other members of their species, as we too have done for millennia.

One Sunday in November 1822, a man named William Cobbett also travelled through Doscomb on horseback. He recorded the journey as part of a series published in the *Political Register* newspaper, which was later turned into the better-known book *Rural Rides*, which is still in print today. His description of the route was vague, but local historians believe he crossed over the main road from Petersfield to Winchester before, upon asking directions to Hawkley, he rode up into the 'pretty green lane' through which I, too, was now riding two centuries later. I couldn't tell how much the lane had changed in that time – whether the same trees and hedgerows lined the verges or if they had been cut down and regrown since then. But Cobbett himself described the lane that day as the most interesting 'that ever passed in all his life', recalling one moment in particular that seems to have buried itself in his memory. It's the kind of moment many of us experience from time to time, when we are struck so suddenly by the beauty of nature that all we can do is surrender to it. Cobbett wrote:

> The lane had a little turn towards the end; so that, out we came, all in a moment, upon the very edge of the hanger! And never, in all my life, was I so surprised and so delighted! I pulled up my horse, and sat and looked; and it was like looking from the top of a castle down into the sea, except that the valley was land and not water.

Cobbett's journey took place in late autumn. Musing on the view that surrounded him, he wrote that 'while the spot is beautiful beyond description even now,' he could only imagine what it must look like in spring, 'when the trees and hangers and hedges are in leaf'. Now here I rode along the same path, and in that same season of his imagination, a woman and horse born of a world so changed from his that it would make him reel. To me, it was still as beautiful as he hoped it would be, albeit with less birdsong and more traffic. Even here on this barely used road, I passed a sad, squashed traffic cone and a sign warning motor vehicles away from the woods – constant reminders that cars now rule modern highways.

The road ended, and a narrowing of the track that marked the start of the bridleway. It was so quiet that the contrast was barely noticeable, but the bridleway felt different. A haven, tucked away from the unpredictable world of cars and motors. Nature is never predictable, but the rhythms and cycles of woodland are comforting – the assurance, as Rachel Carson wrote in her 1962 book *Silent Spring*, that morning follows night and spring comes after winter. We can root ourselves in these cycles if we choose to. We can be a part of something greater than ourselves; find solace and stability in the natural world, and let go of the many things we cannot control. Moving into a space like this, away from the realm of the humanmade, reminded me of what was truly sacred. Peace, birdsong, the scent of life. As Roxy and I travelled deeper into the trees, the hum of bumblebees was replaced by that muffled quietude you only find in woodland – a stillness infused with creaking growth. Blackbirds sifting through leaf litter, always just out of sight. A nuthatch tapping against bark. The melancholic mewing of a buzzard in the sky, mobbed by crows. These were the sounds of a landscape reawakening after the long, dark winter.

A short distance from the Warren, in a stretch of woods known as the Ashford Hangers, a signpost marked a spot now known as Cobbett's View. The story goes that this spot was overgrown with shrubs for several decades until the council realised a trig point was buried underneath it and cleared the area to reveal a beautiful view of the surrounding countryside. They paired the spot with Cobbett's description of the landscape and labelled it accordingly. Yet, after poring over old Ordnance Survey maps and using my limited millennial knowledge to retrace his route, I couldn't help feeling this was not the viewpoint he was referring to. Not that it took away from the beauty of the spot – and it was close enough that the view would be geographically similar and equally lovely to stumble upon. But I was convinced his 'top of a castle' moment had been in the lane I had just travelled through, followed by his descent through Doscomb, which sounded all too familiar. He described the steep, slippery chalk track as like marle – a loose, crumbling earth that he rightly claims is like 'grey soap' when wet. Upon asking a local woman for directions to Hawkley, she tries to persuade him not to ride down the combe as it's too dangerous. Although he manages to complete the journey, he notes how the horses took the lead, creeping down 'partly upon their feet and partly upon their hocks'.

Having ridden here before on an autumn afternoon like Cobbett's, I knew what a 'bad' bridleway could look and feel like. One morning, a few weeks before my wedding, Roxy and I rode out to Hawkley before returning to the livery along a bridleway called Cheesecombe. The weather had been uncharacteristically stormy for that time of year, and that week, a few strong gales had brought trees and branches down around the area. As we wandered slowly back, I noticed a branch had come down ahead of us and was dangling over the path. It's an effort to swing down off a horse and climb back up again without a mounting block, and the branch didn't seem to be hanging too low, so I decided to lay my head down on Roxy's mane in the hope I could squeeze us both underneath the branch and continue our journey.

Unfortunately, I was wearing a body protector – a life-jacket-shaped device that isn't always comfortable to wear but is, undoubtedly, more comfortable than a broken back. As we squeezed underneath it, the branch slipped over my head but caught on the neck of my body protector, and in the few seconds it took for Roxy to push forward and release it, the tugging sensation made her spook, and I fell off. The ground was soft, and I rolled onto my side, slightly winded, but to my horror, I looked up and realised Roxy's reins had caught on the tree, and rather than walking forward, she was now retreating to where I lay on the ground. To this day, I still physically shudder at the memory of her huge rump closing in on me like a big, white moon. Before I could move, one of her hoofs stepped onto my leg. I felt the weight of an entire adult horse squeeze down onto my inner thigh before she hopped back off apologetically and moved forward again. I somehow managed to stand up and walk her back along the path, using a stone wall to clamber back on, and we eventually made it back to the livery an hour later. After a trip to the hospital, I learned nothing was broken or badly damaged, but I had a beautiful horseshoe-shaped bruise for weeks, and there's still a lump of grizzle on the inside of my thigh that I think is there for good. At least I didn't have to walk down the aisle in a plaster cast – every cloud.

In the UK, horse riding has primarily become a recreational hobby rather than a means of travel or industry. Despite this, the economic value of the equestrian sector is still impressive, according to the British Equestrian Trade Association (BETA). It estimates the equestrian industry contributes £4.7 billion of consumer spending to the economy, with around 27 million people in Britain claiming to have an interest in horses. And although horse riding today is mainly reserved for pleasure or sport and can sometimes be associated with a particular social class, you don't have to look far to see how deeply horses were once woven into everyday society.

Surely almost all of us will have bought a pint from a pub called the White Horse, the Plough, the Nag's Head, the Fox and Hounds, or the Coach and Horses? It's possible you were in a farming village, where men once gathered at the end of a long day of ploughing the fields with their horses. Or you may have been on a popular hunting route, where the riders would dismount for a drink after a morning in the field. Or more than likely you were in an old coaching inn, an echo of life before railways and motor cars replaced the horse-drawn stagecoach. Cities, towns and villages in the UK are replete with equestrian clues that reveal how much we once relied on the domesticated horse in our daily lives. In my home town of Petersfield, a market town in Hampshire built on the wool trade, we have a coaching inn dating back to the 1600s, a wine bar called the Stables, a blacksmith's forge that has been in business for almost a century and a statue in the town square of William III mounted on horseback.

Away from the towns, rural landscapes have also been shaped by our relationship with horses, etched with reminders of old industries and travellers' paths. Bridleways weave through fields and forests, the connectors of the countryside, and even today, they are still used and treasured by riders, walkers, joggers and cyclists. These pathways were vital to the tradespeople that all relied, to some extent, on horses, which is why old buildings like mills, brick kilns, granaries and oast houses are, in turn, never far from a bridleway. Hampshire is heavily marked by centuries of rural craft, from vineyards and chalk pits to coppiced hazel woodland used to make wattle fencing, thatching spars, walking sticks, fishing rods, baskets, bean sticks and firewood. Shipwrights logged timber from the Hampshire countryside and hauled it down to Portsmouth, and beer was brewed from flowery hop gardens, escapees from which can still be found today growing wild in the hedgerows. Each of these industries relied on some form of horsepower, whether it was carting produce, hauling timber or milling raw materials. When the Industrial Revolution and mass production began to dominate the British economy, the invention of the steam engine and the urban factory saw the more artisan rural trades start to decline. In some parts of the British Isles, bridleways quietly creeping beneath woodland canopies and open skies have become the only proof that these slower and steadier means of production once existed.

Few inventions have had as powerful an impact on the world as the motor car, first patented by German engineer Karl Benz in 1886. The etymology of 'car' originates from either the Anglo-Norman *carre*, Latin *carra*, or Gaulish *karros*, which all roughly translate to 'a two-wheeled chariot or wagon'. The word originally referred to any wheeled horse-drawn vehicle, so when the motorised version was invented, one of its earliest names was the 'horseless carriage'. The popularisation of the car throughout the United States and Europe meant that by the 1930s, horse-drawn carriages had almost disappeared from British cities. It also meant the network of British roads that had, up to now, been maintained for travel by foot, horseback and carriage would be redesigned to cope with the increased traffic brought on by motor cars. Over the twentieth century, country lanes were resurfaced, and we built new roads using asphalt and concrete, making them smoother and safer and allowing them to be busier. Cars became our dominant mode of transport, and while travellers on foot, bicycle or horse were still entitled to use most roads, it became safer for anyone using these slower modes of travel to retreat to those quieter pathways that had woven, undisturbed, through the woods, moors and fields for hundreds of years.

In parallel with the decline in horse-drawn vehicles through the twentieth century, equestrianism primarily became a more recreational activity in the British Isles. Public bridleways, like footpaths, have become spaces of relaxation and exercise. That is good news for anyone drawn to the countryside for peace and escapism, but it also means these routes are now treated differently in terms of their societal use and economic value. Until very recently, many were in danger of disappearing. A plan laid out by the UK government meant that on 1 January 2026, any old footpaths and bridleways that councils had not recorded on official 'definitive maps' as public rights of way would no longer be legally accessible to the public, under a clause in the UK's right-to-roam legislation. The government's plan could have resulted in thousands of footpaths, alleys and bridleways being lost to the public unless councils recorded them on maps before the 2026 deadline. This would have been a particularly catastrophic change for riders, who can already only access 22 per cent of public rights of way.

Fortunately, the deadline was scrapped in 2022, infinitely delaying the plan, an announcement that delighted and surprised the equestrian community. Will Steel, 2026 Project Manager at the British Horse Society (BHS), spoke to me about his organisation's campaign to mitigate the impact of the proposed 2026 cut-off date. Together with other countryside access organisations like the Ramblers, Open Spaces Society and Cycling UK, before the 2022 announcement, their best hope had been to delay the implementation of the proposed plan for at least a few years. Their joint campaign had been built on the organisations' shared beliefs that all public pathways, including bridleways, are an essential element of the British landscape and should remain accessible to anyone who wants to use them responsibly.

For one thing, they are places of safety. 'At the most basic level,' Will explained, 'the existing network of bridleways and byways is limited and not well connected, forcing equestrians to use sections of busy roads whenever they wish to ride out. According to BHS figures, since 2010, 44 riders and more than 440 horses have been killed in traffic accidents. Recording many historic routes provides vital links within this network and enables riders to use safe, off-road routes much more easily.' Will also pointed to the recent COVID-19 pandemic as an example of why access to outdoor spaces is so vital for our wellbeing: 'The succession of lockdowns and restrictions we all experienced emphasised the value of being able to access and enjoy nature and green spaces, and the rights of way network is key to this. Enabling people – riders or otherwise – to unlock a network of rights of way local to them brings physical and mental benefits.'

And it's not only individual riders and horses that benefit from bridleway access. An improved network of bridleways and byways provides a vast opportunity for people to choose more environmentally sustainable modes of transport for a variety of journeys, particularly as people do not have to be on horseback to enjoy the benefits of a bridleway. With no stiles to manoeuvre and gates at least five feet wide, equestrian routes are also incredibly accessible, making them particularly suitable for those wishing to access the countryside using mobility vehicles or families with buggies or young children. 'With appropriate management,' Will explains, 'not only are these routes available for recreational use by people close to their homes, they also provide opportunities to make more purposeful journeys, such as commuting, shopping and doing the school run, instead of relying on private car use.' Economically, the equestrian industry in the UK generates billions in consumer spending, estimated to be around £5,548 per horse, according to one 2019 study by BETA. This economic boost benefits the local communities where equestrian activities are encouraged to thrive. An improved equestrian rights-of-way network only makes it easier and more enjoyable for these local economies to benefit.

Aside from the health-related, sustainability and economic benefits, Will explained how bridleways and other public access paths deserve our protection for their historical and cultural value. 'The routes we are seeking to record and protect provide a fascinating insight into local history and inform and shape our knowledge and appreciation of the landscape. They are often significant landscape features – old hedged green lanes, sunken tracks marking old field boundaries, routes on which we find beautiful old pack-horse bridges, boundary markers and mileposts. The research carried out as part of recording the UK's bridleways has been incredibly interesting and addictive and it highlights the value of our archives and record offices across the country.' Regardless of changing government plans, members of the public who share a love for these old pathways can still make a massive difference in the movement to protect them, as Will explained: 'The routes we are seeking to protect are, by definition, currently unrecorded and thus vulnerable to development, obstruction or simple neglect in the future. So Project 2026 will continue in some form, and we welcome anyone interested in taking part.' The BHS runs training courses to explain the work they want to do and demonstrate the tools members of the public can use to help them with it. It also encourages people to plot routes on its website that they wish to have officially recorded by their local authority, including offering help with researching, gathering and collating evidence.

Despite the government scrapping the 2026 deadline, like many people, Will is still wary about the future of public access. The legislation that originally introduced the deadline provided breathing space for a possible delay of up to five years, but even that was contested by a handful of groups who were opposed to any delay at all, including the National Farmers' Union and the Country Land and Business Association. Will warned that these organisations were now lobbying for the government to change their position and reinstate the cut-off once again. 'What the government announced is its intention to repeal the legislation,' he explained, 'but until the repeal happens, we have to remain cautious.'

Bridleways are only one type of public access path in the UK. Unless there is a sign nearby to distinguish them, they can look like any other public footpath, permissive path (one whose use the landowner permits) or restricted byway (a path open to walkers, riders, cyclists and any non-mechanically propelled vehicle). Local highway authorities maintain bridleways as they would any other paths but have to consider a few additional factors. Aside from making them stile-free and as wide as possible, they must remove overhanging branches and other obstructions to make room for the minimum height of a mounted rider, which is around two and a half metres above ground level. The ground must also be suitable for carrying the extra weight. The average horse weighs about 500kg, while a horse's hoof can measure up to 250mm wide. Depending on the horse's pace, only two hooves might be in contact with the ground at any given time, which means all of that 500kg weight is concentrated in a tiny area. Boggy ground and large holes can cause horses serious strains and injuries, while both stony ground and dry, cracked mud can damage the soft soles of their hooves.

In the UK, the maintenance of public rights of way is the responsibility of the local highway authorities who, according to the Highways Act 1980, have a duty to 'assert and protect the rights of the public to the use and enjoyment of any highway for which they are the highway authority, including any roadside waste that forms part of it.' They are further obliged to 'prevent, as far as possible, the stopping up or obstruction' of a public highway, and it is within this detail that the issue of preserving footpaths has become the most tangled. Of the estimated 91,000 miles of footpaths, 20,000 miles of bridleways, 2,300 miles of byways and 3,700 miles of restricted byways across the UK, around 9 per cent are either impassable, blocked off or effectively unusable, according to a 2016 survey by the Ramblers Association. Problems range from routes being blocked by barbed wire and electric fences, to broken stiles and dense, impenetrable undergrowth. I knew from my experience with Roxy how a simple overhanging branch could prove incredibly difficult to pass, and it's easy to deduce how encountering even the smallest amount of barbed wire or broken fencing along a route can be enough to discourage the public from exploring their local area, especially those already living with mobility issues.

Not all bridleways are in rural areas, of course. Even the busiest of Britain's towns and cities have public rights of way for equestrians, one of the most famous being Rotten Row in London's Hyde Park. This sandy stretch of designated bridleway running along the south side of the park was not always the peaceful, relaxing spot it has become today. More than 300 years ago, it was a hotspot for highwaymen, who targeted victims as they travelled between Kensington Palace and Whitehall. In 1690, King William III ordered the route to be lit by 300 oil lamps so his courtiers could travel more safely, making it one of the first lit highways in England. The road became known as the Road of the King, or *Route du Roi* in French, which was then corrupted to its present name of Rotten Row. By the beginning of the eighteenth century, it had become a fashionable and popular meeting place for London's upper class, who walked, rode and drove carriages up and down the park. Today, riders will use it, either riding their own horses or, more commonly, taking riding lessons from the commercial stables nearby. The Household Cavalry Mounted Regiment also use it – they have exercised their horses there since 1795 – as do the six police horses that are stabled in the Old Police House nearby.

The value of a bridleway, like so many aspects of the great outdoors, can, if necessary, be pinned down to statistics. These days it is simple to measure economic growth, visitor numbers, health benefits and all the other factors associated with enjoying open spaces. Those statistics are vital for driving positive change from the people in power who perhaps view the world through a different lens, a lens less focused on sentimental impacts and more on financial ones. This is, after all, the kind of world we have built for ourselves, where almost everything must be quantifiable if it is to be protected. With that expectation comes the need to encapsulate our relationship with nature within a single data set, document or Zoom call. The truth is that nothing can replicate the experience of stepping onto a green lane that has been etched into the landscape and inked onto faded, yellow maps for centuries. The scent of fallen leaves among bluebell shoots; wild garlic bulbs unearthed by badger snout; the gentle *clip-clop* of a horse and rider enjoying the first light of a late summer morning. These 'wilder' pockets of space, especially those away from busy roads, have become liminal havens where the human and non-human can co-exist, side by side.

All public rights of way are precious, but bridleways, in particular, are places where the domesticity of humans interweaves with the wildness of the natural world, facilitated by that most gentle and intelligent of animals, the horse. We like to think we are separate from nature, but of course, this is illogical and untrue. Any difference we invent between our species and the rest of the animal world is a mere matter of perception, which is perhaps why horse riding feels so powerful for so many people, including me. Horses are the perfect intermediary between us and the rest of nature. We like to believe we have tamed them and controlled them, and in many ways, we have. But deep down, beneath the saddles, dressage tests and haynets, horses cannot deny their more primitive selves – and neither can we. Riding on horseback reveals a wilder side to our overly managed landscape. And in doing so, we open a line of communication with an animal that, for hundreds, if not thousands, of years, has allowed us to sit on its back and be carried along quiet lanes and over windswept hills, through frothing streams and down into moss-damp dells.

Horses and the pathways left open to them, not only connect us to the earth we walk on together, but they also bring us closer to our true selves, and to our heritage. Our stories and histories are woven into these pathways, memories reverberating around our green lanes. They remind us of how we have shaped the world, for better or worse; how we have connected with our communities over time; how we have pursued our instinctive needs to travel, to seek food and shelter, socialise and form relationships. To keep these spaces full of memory, all we must do is tread the same paths, either on foot or by hoof. The beauty of a bridleway is in the strand of horsehair caught in a barbed wire fence, the hoofprints pressed into the soil or even the horseshoe that lies dented and abandoned in the bluebells, dislodged by stone or kick or canter. Something about these quiet pathways that allows us to feel like we are treading more gently on the earth. And perhaps that is because, on horseback, we do not tread directly on the earth at all; instead, a wiser creature that knows nothing of our modern-day conflicts carries us, concerning itself only with the sun and moon and stars, the sound of water, the taste of grass, and whether or not that pesky road sign has moved two inches from where it was before.

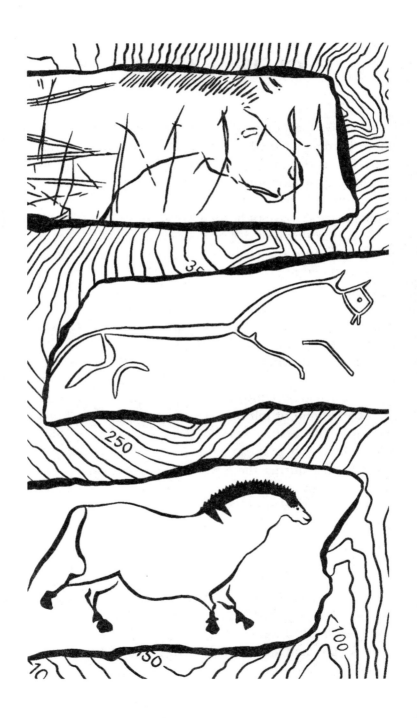

CHAPTER TWO

Chalk and Bone

A dozen red kites dipped and swerved over a stubble field whose borders writhed with dried rosehips and old man's beard. It was the first bright day in January after weeks of rain, and a quarter moon waxed high against the winter sun. Everything felt renewed; the year, the sky and the cold, gentle breeze. A wave of freshness broke over the hilltop as I stood, gazing down at a leaping, sweeping horse that had been carved into the chalk slopes of the Berkshire Downs 3,000 years before.

At such a close distance, the Uffington White Horse could be any other path scratched into the hillside, albeit brighter than the foot-churned track we had walked up to get here, which was grey with mud, pawprints and sheep droppings. From where I stood, I could only see the eye and ear, pressed into the earth by human hands, coarse winds and the unyielding whisper of time. The Uffington horse is one of a handful of hill figures scattered across the English landscape. The best view of it is from across the Vale of White Horse, where it can be seen from 20 miles away. It is so bright that during the Second World War, it had to be covered in turf and hedge trimmings so Luftwaffe pilots couldn't use it for navigation. It measures 365ft long and 130ft tall, with a single flowing line running from nose to tail, a beaked head, and a large, round eye spreading 4ft across the grass.

Contrary to popular belief, this galloping figure was not etched into the ground but formed by digging a trench and filling it with crushed chalk. Every summer, a group of volunteers spend a weekend 'scouring' the horse to keep the figure bright and clean by beating fresh chalk into the surface, a tradition that dates back centuries. Scouring was once such an important part of life in the Vale that the landowner was obliged to organise the ceremony and feed and entertain the diggers. There would be musicians, horse races, free-flowing food and alcohol; in 1843, the landowner even brought in a circus, and the elephant van got stuck trying to drive up the hill. During the scouring ceremony, a ballad was sung by merrymakers in Berkshire dialect to rouse the diggers:

The owl White Horse wants zetting to rights,
And the Squire hev promised good cheer,
Zo we'll gee un a scrape to kip un in shape,
And a'll last for many a year!

The scouring ceremony lapsed after 1857, and by 1880 the horse was so overgrown that it was almost invisible to those who didn't know where it was supposed to be. It was cleaned and recut four years later, but by 1894, it was smothered in weeds again. Fortunately, the tradition has since been reinstated (with less alcohol) under the guardianship of the National Trust and English Heritage, and the horse shines bright and clear over the green valley. But why was it carved in the first place?

Like so many ancient landmarks, nobody is entirely sure why the Uffington White Horse exists, although there are a few convincing theories. Standing at the top and looking down, it's obvious a figure like this was meant to be visible from a distance, which supports the popular idea that it was a tribal banner or badge to represent the people of the Vale of White Horse below. Why a white horse was chosen is unclear – the Vale was named after the figure, not the other way around. There is plenty of evidence of animal worship in the Bronze Age, with the horse symbol, in particular, appearing repeatedly. There is also a strong resemblance between the Uffington horse and horses that appear on the back of Celtic coins, although the former's beaked head and long tail have also given rise to the idea that the Uffington horse is not a horse at all, but a dragon. However, this theory is not widely supported, as documents that date back almost 1,000 years refer to the figure as a horse.

But like all good stories, the story of the Uffington horse isn't entirely dragon-less. One legend claims the figure is the steed of St George and that the flat-topped hillock directly below the horse, known as Dragon Hill, is where he killed the beast, its spilt blood marked by a bare patch of chalk on the summit. J.R.R. Tolkien's son, Christopher, believed that Dragon Hill was also the inspiration for Weathertop in his father's novel *The Lord of the Rings*, where the leader of the Ringwraiths stabs Frodo. To the west, the land is cut into a series of glacial terraces known as the Giant's Stairs, and a deep combe called the Manger sweeps up to Uffington Castle, an Iron Age hillfort sitting at the top. The area may have even been the site of Iron-Age rituals associated with the horse and castle, while others claim the carving was a celebration of King Alfred's victory over the Danes at the Battle of Ashdown. Some locals swear the horse is slowly moving up the hill; others believe standing on its eye and turning around three times will bring them good luck.

A mile west of the horse is an early Neolithic long barrow known as Wayland's Smithy, named after the godlike blacksmith from Germanic mythology. According to legend, if you left your horse tethered outside the barrow, together with a small coin, Wayland would reshoe your horse while you were away. The path that connects the chalk horse and the Smithy is an 87-mile ancient track called the Ridgeway and is considered Britain's oldest road, used by travellers, riders, herders and soldiers for at least 5,000 years. It is a passage moulded by time, pressed and padded by foot, hoof and paw as one generation after another made their way through beech shades and chalk climbs.

I stood and watched the sheep grazing below the horse's chest, speckled across the landscape like tiny pieces of chalk. When the writer G. K. Chesterton walked out one morning to have a go at sketching the Downs, he first cursed himself for forgetting his stick of white chalk, the shade of which, he believed, was not an absence of colour but 'a shining and affirmative thing … when it grows white-hot, it draws stars'. There was something about this horse that cast an enchantment over the hillside; this living, breathing artefact, marked out by ancient hands in the act of sweet creation. The carving we see today is not the same as the day it was completed by the first diggers. The grass had grown and wilted, the chalk eroded and rescattered, and the movement of life had rippled through and altered it. But at the same time, it was an unbroken path to the past. The rain should have washed it away, the turf should have covered it. But instead, it had been redrawn again and again, a proclamation of love from the people of the Vale. Chesterton, too, would appear to have felt the same when he:

> … stood there in a trance of pleasure, realising that this Southern England is not only a grand peninsula, and a tradition and a civilisation; it is something even more admirable. It is a piece of chalk.

The wind grew colder, I was reminded of William Horwood's *Duncton Wood*, a novel about a community of moles and their worship of England's standing stones. Towards the end of the story, the moles visit Uffington, the place of the Holy Moles, and sleep beside the Blowing Stone at the bottom of the slope, a real sarsen stone full of natural holes that produce a booming sound when blown in the right direction. *Duncton Wood* was my husband's favourite book as a child, and he has loved moles ever since. They seemed to be flourishing here, mounds of soil pushed up in every direction across the hilltop whose steep, rippling slopes were shaped by the retreating permafrost from the last Ice Age.

Around the chalk horse that had watched over the valley for 3,000 years, there were newer marks on the earth. Fresh prints from a horse's hoof, dark with winter dew, ran in lines along the path; evidence of a warm, breathing horse beside its cold, white counterpart. Here and there, a hoof had churned up the grass to reveal the soil beneath. I wondered how many seeds slept underground, waiting for the warmth of early spring to burst out of their beds and unfurl towards the sky. Chalk and limestone soils are known for their wildflower diversity. I closed my eyes and imagined what might be growing here in a few weeks: feathery blossoms of yarrow, pincushions of field scabious, and the violet petals of meadow cranesbill. And later, high above it all, the impossible sound of a swift drifting through the air, screaming the arrival of summer.

This was the kind of place where time travel felt possible, as though there were a thin veil draped over the Downs bluring together past, present and future. The nineteenth-century writer Thomas Hughes was local to Uffington; he was a keen advocate of the scouring and restoration of the white horse, and of keeping England's traditions alive:

> ... to bring to life in us the feeling that we are a family, bound together to work out God's purposes in this little island, and in the uttermost parts of the earth; to make clear to us the noble inheritance which we have in common; and to sink into their proper place the miserable trifles, and odds and ends, over which we are so apt to wrangle.

Some things should be allowed to slip into the past, but I was obliged to agree with Hughes on this one. The existence of this horse came from choices made to connect with the earth and each other. The act of scraping back the weeds and adding new chalk to old, laughing in the sun and wind that has swept over this hillside for 3,000 years or more. This was a living, breathing artefact, not a relic behind glass in a museum, and it needed constant attention to be kept alive, revived and reborn year after year. And like the rest of the landscape – like the essence of nature itself – the Uffington horse relied on the inevitability of change to keep its heart beating.

As I left the horse on the hilltop, a noise made me glance up and notice a raven, croaking and *cronking* just a few feet above me. It soared down over the chalk and circled round and round, its tar-black feathers and crooked beak gleaming, one eye staring down from its invisible tower in the sky. And then it turned away, flipped itself over in a barrel roll, swooped, dipped and somersaulted in mid-air. It was one of the most joyful things I'd ever seen; a ritual in the wind, as old and young as the rising sun. I watched for a few minutes longer, stole one final look at the carving and left the horse and raven together, dancing to the swing of the grass and the ancient beat of the chalk.

U

One summer morning in 1876, a group of archaeologists entered a cave in a leafy limestone gorge on the border of Derbyshire and Nottinghamshire. They had cut a trench through the pile of rocks that blocked the entrance, which opened into one of a series of horizontal caves that penetrated the steep and rugged cliffs known as Creswell Crags. Inside, the archaeologists found what they believed to be the bones of lions, spotted hyenas, Irish elk, Arctic hare, mammoths, sabre-toothed tigers, rhinoceros, wolves and bears, as well as flakes of quartzite and ironstone worked by human hands, bone needles, awls, scrapers and other tools.

Among these fragments, hidden within a layer of fine red loam, they also found one of the oldest pieces of figurative art ever discovered in Britain. It became known as the Robin Hood Cave Horse.

The Robin Hood Cave was named after the legendary outlaw who was said to have avoided capture by hiding inside. While Robin Hood may have been fictional, archaeologists have proven hominids sought out this particular cave over the last few millennia. Evidence shows Neanderthal occupation until about 40,000 years ago, then the presence of *Homo sapiens* from around 22,000 years ago until the end of the Ice Age and beyond. They left behind a wide range of tools and animal bones, including a horse rib that had been intricately engraved into the image of a horse's head. The rib, intentionally grooved and snapped at one end and broken at the other, bears the likeness of the forequarters, head and neck of a galloping horse, with a strong jaw and upright, bristling mane. It is the only identified piece of Upper Palaeolithic figurative art depicting an animal species native to Britain. There must have been something about Creswell Crags that inspired equine art because they were also a favourite location of the artist George Stubbs, who painted a series of equine portraits and landscapes with the Crags as a backdrop, a century before the engraved horse rib would be excavated.

According to the British Museum, in whose archives the rib is now stored, the carving is estimated to be around 12,500 to 13,000 years old. That means it was carved before humans domesticated horses (around the Bronze Age), so the image is one of the only surviving depictions of a wild horse in the world. Today, when we think of wild horses, we might imagine the brumbies of Australia, the mustangs of Nevada or the ponies of the Welsh mountains. But are these animals wild? And if not, are there any genuinely wild horses left on Earth? The answer lies in genetics, but it is still a contentious topic among those trying to crack the code.

The earliest known ancestors of the modern horse were small, dog-sized animals that lived in North America around 55 million years ago. According to the fossil record, they had four fingers on their front legs and three toes on their back legs, and led a peaceful, herbivorous life eating small herbs and bushes. Grasslands had not yet developed, so these ancient animals did not graze like the modern horse. After the dinosaurs had become extinct 10 million years before, there was an explosion of mammal species due in part to the warm, jungle-like climate, including the ancestors of the rhinoceros and tapir, both of which are genetic cousins of the equids (a mammal of the horse family). When grasslands finally developed, and the landscape opened up, horses evolved to become more adapted to speed. Their toes merged into one hoof, their legs grew longer, and their leg joints began to swing backwards and forwards rather than rotating, which lengthened their stride. Through these adaptations, horses benefited from their size and speed together with stamina and endurance, a combination not commonly found in mammals of their stature.

Around 14 million years ago, the climate began to cool again, and what had been a savannah-like landscape became temperate grasslands that could not support as many species. Fortunately, horses had crossed the Beringia land bridge, a grassland steppe between the Chukchi Peninsula of the Russian Far East and the Seward Peninsula of Alaska, and avoided extinction. However, many herbivorous mammals went extinct as a result of the change in climate, and by the end of the Pleistocene, horses had disappeared from the fossil record in North America. During the Ice Age, the sea level had fallen by several feet (possibly due to so much water being locked up in glaciers). This drop exposed the ocean floor and enabled many plants, animals and humans to migrate back and forth across the two continents. Through luck and adaptation, the modern genus *Equus* became the only survivor of the equine lineage, spreading across the world and becoming one of the most abundant large mammals on land.

The first relationship between humans and horses was one of predator and prey. In Europe, *Equus* was one of the most hunted species alongside bison and reindeer, and by the Neanderthal period, between 150,000 and 40,000 years ago, early humans ate horses. Neanderthals hunted them so heavily that horse populations became increasingly fragmented across Europe until they were almost at risk of extinction for a second time. Like so many other megafauna, including the mammoth, woolly rhinoceros, Irish elk, cave bear and aurochs, horses struggled to adapt to the changing climate and growing human population. But in a twist of fate, the tribes of humans that had helped drive them to near extinction would also be responsible for their salvation, leading to a relationship never seen between humans and the rest of the animal kingdom.

Nobody is sure when humans first domesticated horses; there is no clear evidence in the archaeological record, although the Bronze Age seems to be a good guess due, in part, to artistic depictions of people on horseback — the first equestrians. Some of the strongest evidence has been gathered from one particular site in northern Kazakhstan, where a culture of people now known as the Botai lived near the banks of the Iman-Burluk river around 5,500 years ago. Excavations of their settlements revealed large numbers of horse bones, despite the Botai not being nomadic people, suggesting that wild horses were captured and then raised for meat rather than being hunted on the move. Fat residues in pottery have also been identified as horse milk, so the Botai must have been on reasonably good terms with their captive horses (as anyone who has milked an animal knows).

But it wasn't just meat and dairy that drew the Botai to domestication. On examining the remains of the horses' teeth, archaeologists discovered a band of wear on the edge of one of the premolars where the enamel had worn away. The only way this pattern could have formed is by regularly placing an object in the horse's mouth, which could mean these horses wore some form of mullen (a piece of metal that forms part of the bit), used to make contact with and control the horse's head. So it is likely the Botai were not only farming their horses but were riding them, too.

By the end of the Bronze Age, a wave of human migration had swept across the globe. This mass migration was undoubtedly assisted by the domestication of the horse, which changed how people ate, farmed, hunted, travelled, worked and waged war. However, the intensive breeding of horses did not begin until the eighth or ninth centuries, when the Islamic conquest of Spain and the English crusades introduced Arabian stock into Europe. Arabians were a fast, striking breed, and their arrival encouraged breeders to set up proper studs, often to produce warhorses. This breeding intensified further in the late medieval period, and the more modern types of horses we are familiar with today started to emerge. Breeding introduced weaknesses as well as strengths, however. The reduction in genetic diversity caused health problems that are still common in modern horses.

The modern horse was pushed to the edge of extinction and brought back again by human hands, and the price horses paid was to be tamed, farmed and made subservient to their new masters. But what of the wild horses that evaded domestication? Small pockets of horses survived until they were finally rounded up across the centuries, including the Eurasian wild horse, known until recently as the tarpan, which became extinct in 1909 when the last specimen died in captivity in Russia. It is unclear, however, if these were a genuine wild species or if they were just feral or hybrid horses. The death of the last Eurasian wild horse might have signalled the end of the species entirely, if it wasn't for one other subspecies of horse that had wandered the grassland steppe of Mongolia for thousands of years – a land of extreme temperatures that can reach 40°C in summer and −28°C in winter. This subspecies came so close to extinction that every specimen walking the Earth today is descended from only 14 individuals, taken from the wild, held in captivity and reintroduced back to the steppe decades later. Its name is Przewalski's horse (pronounced *shuh-VAL-skee*), named after the Russian colonel who first collected skull and skin specimens and enabled the species to be formally classified. Fortunately for me, there is more than a skull and skin to investigate, because a living, breathing herd of Przewalski's horses existed quite happily only 20 miles from my front door.

U

It was a cold, spring morning when we arrived at Marwell Zoo, a wildlife park in Owslebury, just outside Winchester. Having grown up in the same county as Marwell, my husband Dave and I had been here numerous times, but this was our daughter's first visit. Like most children, she loved animals but had never seen anything bigger than a horse in real life, and we couldn't wait to see her expression when she first saw the giraffes in their stables, or the hippos glooping in the mud, or a tiger pacing through the long grass of its enclosure. I have never been able to reconcile the ethical question surrounding zoos, seeing both the benefits and disadvantages of keeping species in captivity. Today, however, I was switching off that part of my brain to see the zoo through my daughter's eyes and enjoy the fact that we were here to see an animal with a truly fascinating history. Somewhere between the gift shop and the tropical bird house, my local herd of Przewalski's horses lived and grazed, blissfully unaware of their palaeontological celebrity status.

Like the Eurasian wild horse, it is unclear if Przewalski's horse is a truly wild horse or a feral hybrid, although many scientists agree it remains the 'best of the rest', meaning the closest we have to the real thing. In their Mongolian homeland, they are known as *takhi*, which means 'spirit'. With an estimated 1,900 individuals alive today, their numbers have recovered since they were first moved into breeding programmes to save them from extinction; all the Przewalski's horses left on Earth are now the direct descendants of specimens captured between 1910 and 1960. Prior to this, they were last seen in the wild during the 1960s in the Gobi Desert, their numbers having plummeted so much due to human interference, including military presence, poaching and capture, that intervention was essential to stop the species disappearing altogether. Threats have now expanded to habitat loss, climate change, low genetic diversity, hybridisation and disease. They are at least now legally protected in Mongolia, and conservation efforts are helping to combat issues and increase population numbers further. These efforts include those of the Smithsonian Conservation Biology Institute, which devised a creative and experimental tracking system by braiding solar-powered GPS transmitters into the horses' tails.

Although long considered to be the last surviving species of wild horse, a recent genetic study has raised speculations on the origins of Przewalski's horse. New data suggests a close genetic relationship between Przewalski's horse and the Botai horses, which some have interpreted as proof that Przewalski's horses were also domesticated before returning later to the wild as a feral subspecies. However, it is possible that Botai horses were merely tamed, rather than domesticated, and there is still no strong evidence proving Przewalski's horses are feral descendants of domestic ancestors.

Even today, the genetics of the Eurasian wild horse continues to be a contested subject. In the years leading up to the Second World War, one German zoologist became so obsessed with its genetic lineage that he attempted to do the impossible: resurrect an extinct species. The zoologist was a man named Lutz Heck, a member of the Nazi party and a close friend of the convicted war criminal Hermann Göring. His brother, Heinz, was also interested in genetic experimentation. Unlike Lutz, however, he did not buy into the Nazis' beliefs. Heinz was even temporarily sent to the Dachau concentration camp for his suspected links to communism and for marrying a Jewish woman. Born to the director of the Berlin Zoo, the Heck brothers' fascination with animals seemed natural, but Lutz's interests took a darker turn than his brother's. Instead of simply wanting to protect and study animals, he hunted and experimented with them. At a time when some zoologists in Europe were trying to breed ligers and tigons, meddling with gene pools and conjuring up new godlike ways to shape the animal kingdom, Lutz decided to experiment with selective breeding to emphasise specific, desirable traits. It was an ideology echoed in the darkest visions of the Nazis in their pursuit of the 'perfect' Aryan race. Lutz shared the Nazi fascination with primeval landscapes, extinct animals and an older and, to the Nazis, 'purer' world that had not only been lost but that they felt needed recovering and returning to its rightful owner, the 'master' Aryan race. Lutz believed that an extinct animal's genes must remain within the gene pool of its closest living species, and that he could concentrate those genes by breeding the animals that looked the most like their extinct antecedents. This theory of back-breeding proved to be fruitless. Even so, it didn't stop him from raiding the zoos of eastern Europe in pursuit of his experiments, including looting the most valuable animals from Warsaw Zoo and slaughtering the rest by way of a private hunting party.

Lutz's efforts included breeding together the mares of Konik, Icelandic and Gotland horses, who he believed

looked visually closest to the extinct species then known as
the tarpan. The name originated when early explorers of
the central Asian steppes saw the wild horses that lived
there and named them tarpans. What they saw was most
likely a hybrid feral horse that had escaped – a relic of wild
horses rather than the real thing. The name has since fallen
out of use among research circles, although it is still
commonly used to refer to extinct wild horses. Concerned,
however, that the horses he bred would be too tame and
domesticated to be dubbed 'wild' horses, Lutz brought in a
different breed of stallion in the hope it might draw out the
more tempestuous characters of the ponies. The stallion he
chose was none other than a Przewalski's horse, which also
provided the desired dun colouration and upright mane
attributed to the tarpan. After the first foal was born in 1933
at the Hellabrunn Zoo in Munich, the breeding programme
continued, and the new Franken-breed became known as
the Heck horse. Many of the resulting horses were then
sent to the Białowieża Forest in Poland to become part of a
hunting reserve for Nazi government officials where, in
line with the Nazi obsession for pure, untouched landscapes,
Lutz and his associates envisioned an idyllic forest where
Hitler's inner circle could hunt and roam in their new
imagined future. Fortunately for us all, this vision did not
materialise, and after the war, the forest was returned to
Polish hands and became the protected wilderness that still
exists today. The Białowieża is still one of the last and
largest remaining parts of the immense primeval forest that
once stretched across the European Plain. And as for the
Heck horses that were sent there, they still exist in a small
herd at the edge of the woods, unaware of their dark and
complicated history but free to graze on the marshes and
wade through the pine-sheltered ponds and ancient grasses
that grow there.

When we arrived at their paddock, it seemed the
Przewalski's horses at Marwell were similar in size and shape

to most of the native species of horse found in the UK. They were located on the outer edge of the park rather than in the busier centre, presumably because, no matter how fascinating their history was, I could understand why many of the visitors might be more interested in the tigers and leopards than what looked like a beige, stocky little pony. We eventually spotted them on the far side of their paddock, just behind the café, where a large swathe of grassland lay in a gently sloping valley. Here they stood in a cluster of five beside a small lake as the sun shifted in and out from behind the clouds, and a sea of light rippled over the grass, casting golden shadows against every blade.

With their dun-coloured coats and thickset bodies, I could see how these horses had become interwoven with the idea of a forgotten, ancient world, especially when I looked at images from the famous Lascaux cave paintings in Dordogne, south-west France. In 1940, a young apprentice mechanic and his three friends slipped into the narrow vertical shaft of a cave that had been closed off from the human world for thousands of years. Inside, they found paintings of large animals marked with iron oxide, charcoal and ochre, believed to have first been painted around 17,000 years ago. Among these images were bulls, aurochs, stags, ibex, bison, cats and bears, as well as the most numerous animal found in the paintings, the horse. These equine shapes take many forms throughout the caves, including one known as the 'Chinese horse', whose hooves are depicted slightly to the back, demonstrating a use of artistic perspective far ahead of its time. Another image shows a horse in full gallop with its mane blowing in the wind while its companion falls over, its legs waving in the air.

The Lascaux caves tell so many stories about the birth of human civilisation – you could google them for hours if you weren't keeping an eye on the time. But what struck me then, as we watched the Przewalski's horses at Marwell, was how similar these animals looked to their painted French counterparts. From their dark, zebra-like manes, short and bristly, to their round, creamy bellies and matching white muzzles, each one even had the same brown stripe connecting their mane and tail. Tucked away from the bustle of the crowds, they seemed as much at home here as on the sun-baked Mongolian steppe. From a distance, they could have even been mistaken for a free-roaming pony on an English moorland, except for the most striking detail of all – their thick, heavy necks. There was no sign of the daintiness found in modern breeds, bred for elegance and poise. These were animals built for the wild, engineered by natural forces to keep warm and tolerate the best and worst of the world's climate. Their colour and stoutness brought them visually closer to donkeys than horses, I felt, if it weren't for the lack of the donkey's floppy ears.

Later on, after admiring the tigers and flamingos and stuffing a blueberry muffin into Olive's hands to help her forget she had missed her nap, we wandered back past the horse enclosure to find that they had now left the field and were munching contentedly outside their stables, just like 'ordinary' horses. Their buckets were filled with carefully chosen feed, and I could smell hay in the air – that universally joyful smell that conjures up summer evenings and boozy teenage parties in fields. It was the smell of warmth and sunshine, but it was also the smell of domesticity. These horses would eat fresh grass in the wild, not hay, and although their feed was probably nourishing them equally well, there was something strange about seeing these wild-looking creatures – these cave paintings come to life – in such a domestic setting. They appeared to have everything they needed here to live a long, healthy life; a small herd in which they could express their instincts, an expanse of fresh grass and water, a dedicated keeper and a good supply of food and shelter. They were free from danger and starvation, and like the rest of their species, they had avoided a one-way ticket to extinction. The price of such freedom was to be stripped of their authentic wildness – but then what did it mean to be wild, anyway? Was it a simple scientific label, or was it more profound than that? Something more intuitive, intangible – spiritual, even? A deeper state of being that gave these horses a gleam in their eye I had never seen before, and that made them, according to legend, unrideable?

Przewalski's horses were once considered an Old-World species, which is a collective name for species originating from those parts of the world (Africa, Europe and Asia) that Europeans were aware of before they arrived in the Americas, or the 'New World'. But the reality is that Przewalski's horses descended from dog-sized creatures that first evolved in North America millions of years before they were ever seen in Eurasia. When Christopher Columbus brought the first Spanish horses to the Americas in 1493, he was unknowingly returning them to their ancestral homeland, and although they were by then wholly domesticated, it didn't stop them from returning to the wild in small numbers. The mustangs of Nevada, California, Oregon, Utah, Montana and Wyoming, icons of the Wild West and the pioneering, freedom-seeking spirit of the Americas, all descend from Spanish colonialist horses that either escaped or were set loose. The debate still rages today about whether they are a native species or an introduced invasive species. This debate tends to focus, as they so often do, on conflicts between these feral animals and their farmed counterparts. Opponents of the mustangs claim they are taking up too much land and taking grazing away from cattle and sheep; advocates insist they are filling an ecological niche once taken by their ancestors and that horses graze in a different way to other livestock so they will be drawn to places and plants that other animals avoid.

Either way, when I thought about the representation of wild horses in popular culture – galloping through open plains, untethered and untamed – I could see why the

American mustangs or the brumbies of Australia might capture our imaginations more than the horses that were now munching hay in front of me, basking in the gentle warmth of the Hampshire sun. But at the same time, I felt nothing but peace when I looked at these horses, free from predators and clearly well-fed and watered, just like the zebras we also admired that day, just a few metres away in their paddock. Horse-like in all but their markings, the zebras grazed just as peacefully beneath bowers of trees erupting into spring leaf, the first primroses of the year blossoming at their feet. Perhaps the primroses could detect their exotic heritage and feasted on the African sun radiating from their souls. Or maybe they had just found a suntrap. It is easy to gaze back into the past and long for a return to a different time when these horses were free from persecution and could live and roam undisturbed along the Eurasian steppes. But that wasn't the world we lived in, and as Lutz Heck had proved almost a century ago, we cannot return to the past, only build a new future. Here, at least, this herd of little beige horses could live in peace together, unbothered by my husband, daughter and me standing just a few metres away, enamoured with their stripy knees and round, sandy bellies, and grateful for the fact they still existed here, on Earth, at all.

U

In the early hours of 26 April 1986, a reactor in the Chernobyl Nuclear Power Plant exploded just outside the city of Pripyat in Ukraine. A failed attempt to shut down the reactor set off a nuclear chain reaction so powerful the blast blew the 2,000-tonne reactor lid straight off, emitted 400 times more radioactive fallout than the Hiroshima atomic bomb, and contaminated more than 77,000 square miles of the surrounding land. Almost 40 years later, the site is still deemed too dangerous for people to return there permanently. Despite this, it has become a destination for dark tourism; visitors are drawn to the abandoned classrooms, apartments and iconic Ferris wheel, which, due to open days after the explosion, never carried a paying passenger. The amount of radiation exposure is now estimated to be similar to a long-haul flight, and tour guides have Geiger counters to measure radioactive contamination, just in case.

In this bleak landscape, illuminating an immortal and tragic chapter in the human story, another herd of the world's 2,000 Przewalski's horses roams free through the forests and fields of the Chernobyl exclusion zone. And they are not alone. In the almost four decades since humans were evacuated from the area, it has become abundant with wildlife, including moose, deer, beaver, owls, brown bear, lynx, wolves, ravens, songbirds, birds of prey, and even a flock of swans that have taken to paddling in the radioactive cooling pond. Despite the radiation, they all seem to be thriving, but unlike most of the wildlife that drifted in organically when the humans left, the horses are one of the only species to have been introduced here on purpose.

At the time of the accident, there were no Przewalski's horses living in Chernobyl, and it wasn't until 1998 that the first ones arrived in the exclusion zone. These were a herd of 31 animals, most taken from the Askania Nova nature reserve further south in Ukraine and three more from a local zoo. Spearheaded by conservationists, the project aimed to reintroduce the horses into the exclusion zone in the hope that the lack of humans might provide a sanctuary for the horses to breed and prosper, as it had done for the other species that thrived there. The project, for various reasons, was initially abandoned shortly afterwards, but despite a period of intense poaching in the mid-noughties, the population as a whole continued to multiply. There are now at least 150 Przewalski's horses living and reproducing in the exclusion zone, including within the Red Forest, one of the most contaminated places in the world, named after the ginger-brown colour of the pine trees that died almost instantly from radiation poisoning.

What a strange new Eden for these horses to find themselves in. Not only is the Chernobyl herd thriving, but its members are also one of the only populations in the world that are breeding and expanding by themselves, despite living in one of the most desolate places on Earth. It is difficult to interpret in any other way – these animals appear to be better off living in a toxic, radioactive purgatory than they would be living alongside humans. A few years ago I read *The Sixth Extinction* by Elizabeth Kolbert, a book that, like Rachel Carson's *Silent Spring* and Tony Juniper's *What Has Nature Ever Done For Us?*, permanently changed the way I see our world. In her book, Kolbert argues Earth is in the middle of a modern, humanmade extinction, so catastrophic it is comparable in scale to Earth's five previous extinction events, including a mass eruption of supervolcanoes and a 45,000mph asteroid hitting the planet. Kolbert is one of countless people who believe that humans are having such a devastating impact on Earth's ecosystems that it is driving a new wave of rapid extinction, with estimates already suggesting we are losing species between 1,000 and 10,000 times faster than the natural, baseline extinction rate.

The story of Przewalski's horse is about what it means to be wild, tamed and feral; the consequences of persecuting an animal without restraint; the false belief that we can resurrect the dead; and the joy of pulling a species back from the brink and propelling it, however slowly, into the future. Their survival is a reflection of our fragmented relationship with the natural world. Do we want to be the animal that drags death around, polluting and tarnishing everything we touch? Do we want to live on a planet where other species can only find sanctuary in the poisoned places from which we have exiled ourselves? Przewalski's horse, the wild horse, the tarpan – whichever name we give it – has become a symbol of how we feel obliged to tame nature wherever we go. But if progress means anything, and if the future is a place born from our past mistakes, perhaps we would do well to recognise our proper place on Earth – not as stewards, but as one species among many others, each as deserving of a free and secure existence as the next.

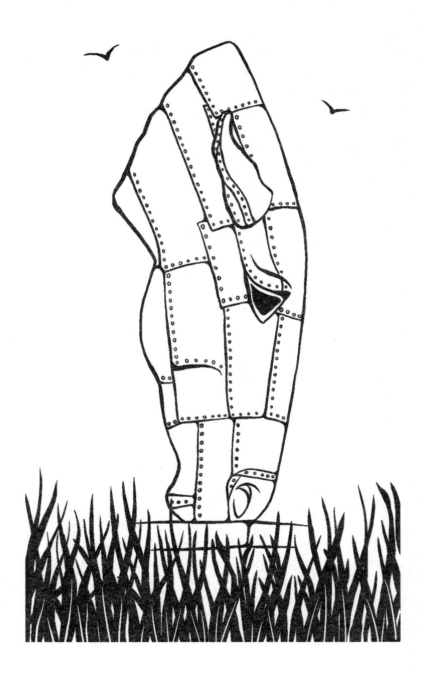

CHAPTER THREE

The Muse

It was early in the day, and the events of the previous two years were still keeping people at home, so when I stepped into the Parthenon, it was quiet, and the air smelled of stone rather than crowds of warm humans. The room in which I stood was long and dimly lit, full of commemorative plaques and information boards. A fragmented marble frieze ran in a band along the central walls, and at the two far ends, rows of larger sculptures stood on display in the shadows. I found the 'start' of the frieze and began to follow it round, reading the note beneath each panel and slowly unravelling the story of this 1,500-year-old relic. It showed a procession of figures celebrating the birthday of Athena, the Greek goddess of wisdom and war, and the beloved patroness of the city of Athens.

Carved into the frieze were a cavalcade of horsemen and their steeds, chariots and riders, men carrying musical instruments, water jars and olive branches, others leading sacrificial animals, here a priestess, there several children, and even a few gods watching the procession, invisible to the mortals surrounding them. As I followed the story, piecing together the broken faces and missing details that were once so intricately carved, I felt like I had joined the procession, too. We were marching, galloping, dancing our way to Athena in the cold half-light of the great hall. But the procession had no end, and the destination was unknown; in the centuries that had passed since this frieze had been carved, the gold and ivory sculpture of the goddess Athena, for whom this cavernous temple had been built, was no longer here. Athena had vanished.

This wasn't the real Parthenon, of course. The real one stood 1,500 miles away on the Acropolis of Athens, much of it destroyed in 1687 when, being used as an Ottoman gunpowder store, it exploded during a siege. Originally built as a temple to Athena, its huge size and lavish use of marble was designed to show off the city's power and wealth when it was completed around 432BC. Today, the design of the building is considered to be impossible to reconstruct, as around half of the original architectural decoration has been lost or destroyed – including the centrepiece of the temple itself, the colossal golden statue of the 'Virgin Athena'. She disappeared from historical record sometime in the first millennium, although luckily there were enough drawings, paintings and copies made to be able to gauge an impression of what she looked like. According to Pliny, it stood around 11.5m tall, with carved ivory in place of her flesh and gold used for everything else, all wrapped around a wooden core. It is estimated the statue cost more to build than the temple in which it stood.

As fabulous as she must have been, I wasn't here to worship the spirit of Athena – and if I were looking for her lost statue, I was miles from her homeland in the warm, sun-drenched mountains of Greece, and even further from Istanbul, where it was rumoured to have been destroyed. Instead, I had come to Room 18 in the British Museum, central London, on a grey January morning, where around half of the surviving Parthenon sculptures were now on display, free of charge, to the public. It was on their arrival in 1816 that they became informally known as the 'Elgin Marbles', a name that has come to embody one of the most controversial questions in the history of the British Museum: who really 'owns' the Parthenon sculptures – or any artefact at all?

At the start of the nineteenth century, a man named Lord Elgin, British Ambassador to the Ottoman Empire, removed half of the remaining sculptures from the ruins of the Parthenon and gave them to the British Museum. According to Elgin, the temple was so dilapidated that the sculptures had to be removed to prevent their total destruction. He also claimed to have acted with full knowledge and permission of the Ottoman authorities, although the Greek government disputes this. They believe Elgin secured permission to investigate the ruins of the Acropolis, but never to strip it of its sculptural decoration, and have since asked for the sculptures to be returned to Greece to be displayed in the newly built Acropolis Museum, 300m from the site of the original temple. It is here that most of the remaining Parthenon sculptures are now displayed, aside from a handful that are scattered across the world in other collections in Paris, Copenhagen, Vienna and Munich. While the return of the statues to Athens would bring most of the remaining sculptures together for the first time in 200 years, the British Museum has denied the request, claiming that:

> The sculptures are part of everyone's shared heritage and transcend cultural boundaries ... The current locations of the Parthenon sculptures allows different and complementary stories to be told about the surviving sculptures, highlighting their significance for world culture and affirming the universal legacy of ancient Greece.

I felt lucky to be able to travel an hour from my home and see the sculptures up close, particularly in a museum that I loved visiting so much. I stood there looking at the fragments, carefully cleaned and displayed. (The sculptures weren't always so well looked after; in the 1930s, museum workmen used copper tools to remove what they thought was dirt, but which turned out to be the honey-coloured patina of the historical surface, resulting in a number of the sculptures being catalogued as 'greatly damaged'.)

But like so many aspects of Britain's past, I found it difficult to justify the museum's claim on the sculptures. It was wonderful that the museum had sought to preserve them all this time, but the fact remained that Athens had asked for them back, and their request had been denied. It made me feel uneasy, as it felt like an echo of Britain's strange colonial assumption that Britain always knows best. And whichever way I looked at it, no matter how grand the room was in which they stood, the collection felt incomplete. I wondered what it would be like for the remaining pieces to be returned and admired all together, reunited after all this time. But I could see the other side, too. The collection was a triumph of the ancient world, and its presence in countries across Europe, including Austria, Denmark, France, Germany, Greece, Italy and the UK, meant its influence could reach even further. Who knows how many people would have been inspired by their visit to Room 18? In fact, if it hadn't been for the sculptures' historical residence in London, one artist might never have encountered them and gone on to create one of the most iconic collections of equine sculptures to have ever decorated the English landscape.

The artist's muse was the last sculpture I came to on my procession around the hall, and the reason I had travelled here at all. Alone on its own plinth in the corner of the room, this was one of the horses belonging to Selene, the moon goddess, who was said to draw her chariot across the sky every night. She is best described in the *Homeric Hymns*, a collection of anonymous poems dedicated to the pantheon of Greek gods:

And next, sweet voiced Muses, daughters of Zeus, well-skilled in song, tell of the long-winged Moon. From her immortal head a radiance is shown from heaven and embraces earth; and great is the beauty that ariseth from her shining light. The air, unlit before, glows with the light of her golden crown, and her rays beam clear, whensoever bright Selene having bathed her lovely body in the waters of Ocean, and donned her far-gleaming raiment, and yoked her strong-necked, shining team, drives on her long-maned horses at full speed, at eventime in the mid-month: then her great orbit is full and then her beams shine brightest as she increases. So she is a sure token and a sign to mortal men.

Her brother Helios the sun god, who drove his chariot across the sky during the day, was said to have four horses, while Selene had only two or three, described by the poet Ovid as 'snow-white'. The sculpture before me (also snow-white, being made of marble) was one of three that had been removed from the Acropolis, with the other two on display back in Athens. A reconstructive drawing showed where it had originally been placed, which explained both its posture and strained expression. It was still beautiful, but without the grace and serenity often found in equine art. With flattened ears, a gaping jaw, flared nostrils and bulging eyes that seemed almost frightened, this horse was clearly exhausted from a hard day's night drawing Selene's chariot. Judging by its position at the far end of the pediment, sinking below the horizon so it had almost disappeared completely, the night was almost over and the dawn about to arrive. At the opposite end, two other horses rose from the marble to welcome the new day and begin their own journey across the sky, no doubt pulling Helios behind them.

As I admired Selene's horse in the dim light, its face scarred and streaked with grey, I felt a breeze against my own skin and looked around to see a door open at the other end of the room. I guessed it was for ventilation, and wondered whether this was the only interaction this horse had enjoyed with the outside world, with nature, with the elements, for hundreds of years. A beast that, imaginary or not, was used to the cold winds of night rushing past its head as it galloped beneath the stars, now entombed behind brick and glass forevermore. It was a striking contrast to another sculpture I had encountered beyond the walls of the museum and the grey, paved streets; one that was inspired by the Parthenon's horse of Selene centuries after its creation, and which greeted me every time I drove up the A3 and into the city of London.

The sculpture, known as the Horse of the South, was made by the artist Nic Fiddian-Green, who has been producing bronze sculptures for over 20 years, specialising in lifelike models of horses' heads. Originally from Ireland, he now lives in Surrey where he uses the horses in his stable block as life models for his work. The Horse of the South is one of many equine sculptures dotted around the country and the world, as some have been purchased for private collections and taken abroad. The one I was most familiar with is located just off the A3, in Surrey, close to the turn-off for Esher, made entirely from beaten lead and weighing close to two tonnes. It takes the shape of a horse's head facing downwards, as if dipping its head into a pool of water, perfectly balanced on the tip of the nose so that, if you put your hand up and hide the fact that the body was missing, the whole thing could simply be a living, breathing horse in its field, caught between enjoying a drink and staying alert.

According to Fiddian-Green, it was conceived as a protest against the urban sprawl of outer London, and, he says it stood 'as a reminder of our roots, when the horse was the only mode of transport within the creation of early London'. The last time I drove past the sculpture (a rarity, as it's far easier to get the train into London from where I live), I saw it twice in the same day; once in the morning, and once after dark on the way back home. By daylight, the lead gleamed under the bright winter sky; a moment of green serenity before the city closed in on us. By night, the sculpture was lit up by a carefully positioned torchlight, shining in the darkness as we slipped back into the rural mosaic of south-east England.

The artist was first inspired by the sculpture of Selene's horse when he visited the British Museum while a student at the Chelsea College of Arts. According to historians, Selene's horse was likely designed by the Greek sculptor, painter and architect Phidias, who also designed the Statue of Zeus at Olympia, one of the Seven Wonders of the Ancient World. Almost 2,500 years later, the ripples of Phidias' art were still drifting quietly through time; the caffeinated commuters whizzing through Surrey were connected, whether they knew it or not, to an ancient world every time they happened to glance at the sculpture on the grassy bank as they zipped past at 70mph. Ancient Athens and twenty-first-century London – two iconic cities that, through the chasm of time, couldn't look more different. And yet here they were, connected by a single idea encapsulated in marble and lead: the recognition of beauty in the form of a horse.

∪

What is it about horses that draws the artists' eye? As an illustrator myself, I knew how satisfying it was to capture the graceful shapes of a horse's anatomy, and as a writer, my love for them led me to writing an entire book about them. Equestrian artistry is such a popular genre that it has a whole community dedicated to it, the Society of Equestrian Artists. It was through this society that I discovered the bold and colourful work of Yaheya Pasha, an equestrian artist whose work is strikingly different to the almost photographic paintings it sits alongside. Expressionistic but with a touch of Fauvism, her application of colour is influenced by artists such as Mikhail Vrubel and Edmund Dulac and her love of manga anime. Passionate about drawing and colour since childhood, Yaheya studied at Central Saint Martins College of Art and Design in London and now creates fine art paintings exploring the form of the horse. I asked her why she had found herself drawn to these animals, and how they had become such an important part of her work: 'Horses have been part of my Indian family background for generations,' she told me. 'My paternal grandfather was a keen horseman and polo player and I have many family members who own horses, so they have always been part of my life and heritage. I suppose it was inevitable they would become my muses!'

Yaheya's real focus on horses began when she was approached by a company that installs art pieces in offices all around the world, changing the displays every two months to inspire both staff and clients, approached her. They asked Yaheya to produce a collection of horse paintings to exhibit in corporate venues in the UK and Europe, which is where her journey took off. She began focusing on the horse as an artistic subject, visiting stables to study and draw them. 'I think horses captivate us through their sheer beauty, energy and sensitivity,' she explained. 'They have their own personalities and are incredibly intelligent. Their movements are filled with grace and dynamism, which makes them a wonder to watch. And this is what I try to capture in my work – their magic and emotion. It's in their faces, their eyes and body language. I think they have a special relationship with us, a kind of symbiotic understanding of emotion and mood. In certain cultures, horses symbolise success – they have certainly brought me joy and happiness as I continue to partner with them on my art adventure!'

As mentioned in chapter two, as far back as prehistory, horses were one of the most common animals found in art, while in the Old English language, there were thought to be at least 16 words for horse, each distinguishing between horses used for carts, luggage, riding, breeding, royalty and war. In Celtic, Roman and Anglo-Saxon cultures, horses even held religious significance. The eighth-century Northumbrian historian Bede wrote how the first Anglo-Saxon chieftains were named Hengist and Horsa, meaning 'stallion' and 'horse' respectively. Many scholars now theorise that these were originally equine deities associated with the

Proto-Indo-European myth of the Divine Twins, figures of youthful horsemen who rescued and healed their people. It has been suggested that these gods were euhemerised (where myths are interpreted as real historical figures and events), just as some Christians believe Jesus was a real man who walked on Earth, rather than being purely symbolic.

One Romano-Celtic goddess, Epona, had a cult following in Iron Age Europe, particularly in Gaul, Germany and countries along the Danube River. Epona (which is also the name given to the fictional horse in *The Legend of Zelda* video games) was the patron of horses, asses and mules, and the Romans used to crown her image with flowers and place it in a shrine within the stables. In the town of Dunstable, on Watling Street (one of the most famous Roman roads in Britain), the bones of 28 horses were found in a well, close to where a Roman posting station used to stand. Posting stations were the Roman equivalent of motorway services, and therefore a common stopping place for horses and riders, but the accumulation of so many bones puzzled the archaeologists who found them; horse meat was not a popular food choice in Roman Britain, as horses were more valuable alive for war, transport and labour. This led to the theory that horses were, in the last few decades of Roman occupation in Britain, seeing a revival in the sacred status they enjoyed under the cult of Epona. As Epona was a deity often associated with chthonic symbols of death and regeneration, the horses found in the well were likely buried whole and with special care, suggesting some kind of supplication to her to protect the dead. Elsewhere, when a Romano-Celtic temple was excavated in Bourton Grounds in Buckinghamshire, archaeologists found a similar burial containing the skull of a horse ringed with oyster shells and crowned with a large, smooth pebble.

Although the Romans came and went, our nation's cult-like fascination with horses remained. When the Anglo-Saxons and Vikings settled here, their reverence of the Norse

gods brought the figure of Odin to our shores, god of
wisdom, poetry, death and magic, together with his eight-
legged horse Sleipnir. According to legend, Sleipnir was one
of Odin's shamanic spirits who carried him through the
Nine Worlds cradled in the branches and roots of the tree
Yggdrasil. He was born when the god Loki shape-shifted
into a mare and became pregnant by the giant stallion
Svaðilfari. Born from the blood of two supernatural beings
– a god and a giant – Sleipnir had the power to move easily
between the realms of the living and dead, which gave him
his name, meaning 'the sliding one'.[1] When he and Odin
were finally killed in battle, he carried Odin to the afterlife,
in keeping with the Norse belief that horses were liminal
creatures in closer communion with the immortal world.
Many believe Sleipnir chose to die when Odin fell, knowing
Odin would not reach the afterlife if he was not there to
carry him. It was this association with the afterlife that led to
horses being used to predict the future, being animals that
were closest to the gods and therefore best placed to
understand them. One method of divination involved
harnessing a horse to a chariot and observing the path they
naturally took, similar to how Boudicca released a hare
before battle to determine her tribe's fortune.

Beyond the English border, horses have also taken centre
stage in the ancient stories of the Scots. In fact, take a visit to
the Helix Park between Falkirk and Grangemouth, and you
will find the largest equine sculptures in the world, towering

---

[1] *Sleipnir* is also the name of the members' magazine for the Icelandic
Horse Society of Great Britain. The Icelandic horse is a hardy, stocky
breed, famous for having two more gaits (the name for how a horse
moves) than most other breeds. As well as the regular walk, trot, canter
and gallop, Icelandic horses can also *tölt*, which is like a smooth, fast
walk, and move at a 'flying pace', similar to the *tölt* but used for racing
rather than long-distance travel. Not all Icelandic horses can perform
both extra gaits; those that can are considered the best of the breed.

above the Forth and Clyde Canal like bewitching, unassailable guardians. Designed by Glaswegian sculptor Andy Scott and measuring 100ft tall and 300 tonnes each, the Kelpies take the form of two steel horses' heads, named after the mythological shape-shifting beasts that were said to inhabit the deepest, darkest lochs and pools, preying on the unfortunate humans that passed them by. One tosses its head to the sky – fierce, flighty and defiant – while the other gazes down in what might look like quiet contemplation if it weren't for the ears, pinned back in concentrated anger. It is this ferocity of the pair's gaze that makes them more kelpie than horse, and like their namesakes, the use of glittering steel allows them to appear both solid and fluid, capturing the mutability of their shape-shifting experience.

The sculpture and its name were designed to reflect the beasts' strength and endurance, which was thought to be the same as 10 regular horses, and to celebrate the transformational change and endurance of Scotland's inland waterways. They appear to spring, suddenly and powerfully, from the lock and basin of the canal they proudly guard; it is an image that triumphs the lineage of the heavy horse, and how it shaped the Scottish landscape through the pulling of wagons, ploughs, barges and coalships along the roads and canals of the Falkirk region. And despite their mythological name, the horses were modelled on two real-life Clydesdales called Duke and Baron. Having been rescued by the charity World Horse Welfare as a two-year-old, Baron lived to the age of 19, spending many years pulling a traditional dray cart in a country park in Glasgow before retirement. His companion Duke worked alongside him, before also being retired. Described by the Kelpies' sculptor as 'patient, well-mannered and the perfect gentlemen', both Baron and Duke were brought to his studio to model for the new sculpture, and now live forever in sparkling steel, guardians of the Scottish waterways.

It is not only the kelpies that have cast their spell on the Scottish landscape – and despite their penchant for human prey, they are by no means the scariest. Much further north, in the Orkney archipelago, a creature known as Nuckelavee was said to dwell in the deep, tempestuous waters surrounding the islands. This horse-like demon was one of sheer evil, with venomous breath that could wilt crops, a black, skinless body and a head 10 times bigger than any human's. In the nineteenth century, a farmer and folklorist called Walter Traill Dennison described Nuckelavee, after meeting another farmer who claimed to have seen him when out walking one night:

> The lower part of this terrible monster was like a great horse, with flappers like fins about his legs, with a mouth as wide as a whale's, from whence came breath like steam from a brewing-kettle. He had but one eye, and that as red as fire. On him sat, or rather seemed to grow from his back, a huge man with no legs, and arms that reached nearly to the ground. His head was as big as a clue of simmons,[2] and this huge head kept rolling from one shoulder to the other as if it meant to tumble off.

Nuckelavee was considered so demonic that some islanders would not even utter his name unless it were followed by a prayer. Like many of the oldest superstitions, Nuckelavee likely helped explain the unexplainable misfortunes of island life, such as crop failures, drownings and disease, and it is probably no coincidence these myths had the strongest presence in places where life could be the most difficult.

One example was the belief that Nuckelavee became enraged by the smell of burning seaweed, common around

---

[2] 'Simmons' is a ball of plaited oat straw, more commonly spelled 'simmens' and measuring around a metre wide.

Orkney during the eighteenth and nineteenth centuries with the rise of the kelp industry. Seaweed had long been gathered by the islanders when it washed up on the shallow beaches or blew in from sea storms, and for centuries, it was spread over the fields as fertiliser. Around 1722, the laird of Stronsay introduced kelp-making to the island, using the traditionally named 'tang and ware' that gathered on the shore (tang grew on the rocks, while ware grew in the sea). When the seaweed was burnt, the ash produced was rich in potash and soda, which were eagerly sought after by the glass and soap industries. Mixed with heather and hay, the kelp fires blazed for up to eight hours before being covered with stones and turf and left overnight. The industry was lucrative – especially for the lairds, who kept around three-quarters of the profits – but it became so prevalent that the islands were described as looking like a volcano. The islanders soon protested that the raging fires' fumes were poisoning livestock, driving away fish, contaminating crops, killing the limpets on the rocks (a source of food in difficult seasons) and making the workers go blind. Arsenic deposits concentrated from the seaweed can still be found in historic burning areas. Burning declined in the nineteenth century, but it is easy to see how closely connected the industry was with the story of Nuckelavee, a creature who became enraged at the stench of burning seaweed and took his revenge on the people who caused it. Nuckelavee was even charged with bringing mortercheyn to the islands, a respiratory disease that mainly affects horses and is more commonly known today as glanders. This highly infectious and deadly condition spread quickly between kelp-producing islands, but as general knowledge about the transmission of infectious diseases did not come about until the latter half of the nineteenth century, the blame was placed on Nuckelavee's wrath, rather than poor biosecurity among the islanders.

Beyond kelpies and skinless equi-demons, who knows how many other stories have emerged from the fierce and graceful figure of the horse? In Greek mythology, the centaurs were mythical creatures, half-horse and half-man, whose famous battle with the Lapiths, known as the Centauromachy, was also depicted on the cold, white walls of the Parthenon. The Greek imagination also gave us Pegasus, the magical, winged horse that sprang from the blood of Medusa when she was beheaded by Perseus, as well as the hippocampus, a lesser-known creature with the upper body of a horse and the lower body of a fish. But there is one magical beast – perhaps the most beloved of all mythical equines – whose roots are buried deeper than all the others.

Nobody is entirely sure where or when the unicorn first came into existence, but the first mutterings came from the Indus Valley Civilisation in the ancient Near East, around 3,000 to 1,300BC. It was here that imagery started to appear depicting a horse-like animal with a single horn protruding from its skull, but it wasn't until ancient Greece that the first written evidence was produced by Ctesias, who was writing a book on India and included one of the first references of what might be considered a unicorn:

> Fleet of foot, having a horn a cubit and a half in length, and coloured white, red and black.

Both of these pictorial and written depictions could have been mistaken for other horned animals like the aurochs or oryx. Pliny the Elder made an attempt in the first century, but his description was a little less magical, and a little more rhinoceros-esque:

> It has the head of the stag, the feet of the elephant, and the tail of the boar, while the rest of the body is like that of the horse; it makes a deep lowing noise, and has a single black horn, which projects from the middle of its forehead, two cubits in length.

It was, however, Pliny's account that gave the unicorn some of its famous character traits, including the inability to be captured alive, an idea that thrived from the medieval period onwards when unicorns became a symbol of, among other things, purity, strength, ferocity, chivalry, chastity and loyalty. According to the seventh-century scholar Isidore of Seville, the unicorn could only be calmed by a flashing virgin maiden:

> The unicorn is too strong to be caught by hunters, except by a trick: If a virgin girl is placed in front of a unicorn and bares her breast to it, all of its fierceness will cease and it will lay its head on her bosom, and thus quieted is easily caught.

Their horns could also purify water, and on emblems and coats-of-arms, they were often shown as collared with a broken chain, signifying their immense power and inability to be tamed. In fact, it was due to this powerful image that the unicorn became the unlikely national animal of Scotland. First introduced to Scotland's royal coat of arms around the mid-1500s, the design originally featured two unicorns facing one another. But when King James VI of Scotland became James I of England, unifying the two crowns, he replaced one of the unicorns with a lion (the national animal of England), as an attempt to display unity between the two countries. If they look closely enough, visitors to Scotland will find unicorns everywhere, from palace gates and market crosses to cathedral sculptures and wooden carvings.

At Stirling Castle, this mythical equine beast has even inspired a 14-year-long historic project to recreate the lost 'Hunt of the Unicorn' tapestries that once belonged to King James V. Dating back to the 1540s, there is no complete record of what happened to the original collection of more than 100 tapestries that once hung in his castle, but an inventory from the time described a set that showed 'the historie of the unicorne'. Using painstaking skill and research, the team resurrected the tapestries with inspiration from the mysterious Unicorn Tapestries, a set of seven French panels dating back to at least 1680, which show the pursuit of a unicorn through the French countryside. With no earlier details of their origins found, these tapestries were looted during the French Revolution, rediscovered in a barn in the 1850s, and have since been studied intensely to learn more about where they came from. Other than the 'AE' monogram appearing in each panel, and the fact they were made in the Netherlands, scholars are still unable to agree who commissioned them and for what occasion. Miraculously still preserved after all this time, the original Unicorn Tapestries now hang in the Metropolitan Museum of Art in New York City, and it was these that helped the team at Stirling recreate those from King James' own collection. Without further evidence, it is impossible to know how close these recreations are to the originals, but the work that went into them demonstrates how the unicorn still manages to capture our imagination, even today. The tapestries have since become hugely influential in popular culture, including appearances in the *Harry Potter* and *Spider-Man* films, and inspiring a 1961 poem of the same name by Leonard Cohen.

U

It is the first morning of May, and drops of warm dew sit heavily among the grasses and wildflowers of the season; sweet violets and corncockles twist their lilac petals between the last of the cowslips; the cuckooflowers wait quietly for the orange-tips. This is the first day of summer, when the Earth and its creatures can dare to dream that the spring rain might have passed, and maybe the sunlight which beams down that morning will linger, just for a while. The sky is full of swifts and swallows, the hawthorns froth with blossom, and if you are very still – and very lucky – you might even hear a cuckoo chiming in the woods.

For the people of Britain, like so many others, May Day is a jubilant time. A day to celebrate the sunlight, the longer days and shorter nights, the season of fertility as the crops grow ripe and rich, and the simple beauty of nature in her most vibrant, flowering months. The celebrations vary from place to place, country to country, but they can all be stripped back to the same ideas, perfectly captured in this simple folk rhyme, sung by generations of schoolchildren in the shift between spring and summer:

> Sing a song of Maytime, sing a song of Spring;
> Flowers are in their beauty, birds are on the wing.
> Maytime, playtime, God has given us Maytime,
> Thank him for his gifts of love, sing a song of Spring.

Even with the scandalous undertones of fertility and 'playtime', May Day was enjoyed by Christians and non-Christians alike (except when it was banned by those party-pooping Puritans during the Interregnum). In England, May Day celebrations have historically included the crowning of a May Queen, dancing around the maypole, folk music, feasting and flowers. May Day also has many crossovers with the Gaelic festival of Beltain, famed for the burning of a huge wicker man to welcome in the summer and evoke divine protection over the cattle and crops. One May Day tradition, however, is a little more eclectic than the others; it is so unusual that it was featured in the final, frenzied scenes of the 1973 British folk-horror film *The Wicker Man*. Its name is the Obby Oss, and despite not being as widely known as maypoles and flower crowns, it has historically been an important part of community life in several English towns, including Barnstaple, Combe Martin, Minehead, Penzance and – most famous of all – Padstow, an ancient fishing town on the north coast of Cornwall. It is in Padstow that the annual Obby Oss festival takes place, a custom carried out by Padstonians for so many centuries that nobody knows exactly when it started, or

who came up with the unique tradition of the Hobby Horse
(pronounced and spelled *Obby Oss* in the local dialect). Like
other May Day festivals, it is thought to have similar roots to
the Gaelic fire festivals, but instead of a burning wicker man
providing the main entertainment, this celebration is all about
the Hobby Horse.

The Hobby Horse is, as the name suggests, technically
modelled on a horse, although you would be forgiven if you
didn't recognise it straight away. Made from a circular
framework with shiny, black material stretched tight around
it, it is carried on the shoulders of a dancer who wears a
grotesque mask and pointed hat to hide his face. A horsehair
tail and a skirt made of the same black material hangs down
from the frame to knee height, and a small, wooden horse's
head, complete with a mane and snapping jaws, sticks out
on the front, attached by a long, straight neck. If you love
the darker, eerier side of English folklore – the kind with
frenzied drumbeats, black paint and Ari Aster-style festivities
– this festival is a dream come true, and it seems just as
popular now as it was when one visitor documented his
experience in 1820:

> There is an annual jubilee kept up at Padstow on May 1st,
> known by the name of the Hobby Horse, in allusion to
> which the inhabitants dress up a man in a horse's skin, and
> lead him through the different streets. This odd looking
> animal amuses, by many whimsical exploits, the crowd
> which follows at his heels, particularly by taking up dirty
> water, wherever it is found, and throwing it in the mouths
> of his gaping companions. These tricks naturally produce
> shouts of laughter, and the merriments are accompanied by
> songs made for the occasion. The origin of the festival
> appears to be unknown.

Two horses take part in the Padstow festival, the Old Oss
and the Blue Ribbon Oss; the latter was introduced in the

nineteenth century by members of a temperance group, in a symbolic attempt to discourage drunkenness during the festival. The festival starts at midnight on the evening before, when the townspeople gather outside the Golden Lion Inn to sing the 'Night Song', a folk song encouraging everyone to rise early the next morning and celebrate the turn of the season. The town is dressed in greenery overnight and flowers are placed on the maypole, and in the morning, the Obby Osses appear in different places and parade through the town, dancing with the crowds to their chants of the 'Morning Song' and trying to 'capture' young maidens under their horse's costume. At last, the two horses meet at the maypole and dance together before returning to their 'stables', and the crowds sing of the Obby Oss' death, knowing he will rise again the following May Eve.

Britain is known for its strange traditions (cheese rolling and bog snorkelling, anyone?), but this is perhaps one of the most unique. You could even go as far as to call it unsettling – the grotesque masks, the wicker man-style echoes of horror (although, to be fair, the festival predates the film, and there is no historical evidence that people were ever burnt alive in wicker men). The capturing of women by the Osses feels particularly uncomfortable, but like all folk traditions, there is also something enchanting about it, which is perhaps why it has survived for so long. A quick search on YouTube shows footage of the festival over several decades, but the festival-goers don't seem to have aged. These traditions are a source of permanence for many of us, particularly nowadays, when it seems like each new year looks almost unrecognisable from the last.

Folklore author Dee Dee Chainey believes observing community traditions that have been upheld for centuries reassures us. By sharing stories from our own past and from that of the people who came before us, we're comforted and reminded that we belong to a community. 'These traditions and customs show us that we are not alone, and that we can rely on the people around us to always be there,' Dee Dee explains. Their repetition also gives us a framework to ground ourselves in, one that tells us who we are and what has come before us. 'They give us hope and direction,' Dee Dee says, 'in what might otherwise be a fear-filled future, filled with unknowns and uncertainties. They make us feel like we belong.'

There is, however, also darkness lurking under the surface of these traditions. When we explore the concept of belonging, this prompts the idea that others are excluded if they do not follow the same traditions or customs. In saying that we 'belong', we can invite in the concept of 'us' and 'them', and this is when folklore can become dangerous. 'Folklore,' Dee Dee explains, 'has been used as a weapon to underpin racist and nationalist agendas in the past.' She emphasises the importance of encouraging everybody to feel included, even when acting out customs and holding festivals, and being mindful of how we might show newcomers, and those who do not want to conform to social norms, how they can still be part of collective cultural stories. 'In that way, we are able to stay rooted within our communities, and still enjoy the traditions that surround us, while ensuring that they no longer enshrine damaging and outmoded beliefs, excluding people purely for the sake of nostalgia.'

Horses are firmly rooted in the British psyche. From the Uffington White Horse hill figure to the Iron-Age chariot burials of Garton Slack and Wetwang Slack, we can see horse-related motifs across the British landscape. I spoke to Dee Dee about the place of horses in British history. 'Horses were symbols of strength, endurance and nobility,' Dee Dee says, 'and the symbol of the horse running through our folklore feeds that national narrative.' As Dee Dee observes, horses have long been woven into the fabric of British folklore, from the legends of warrior kings, like King Arthur, to the tales of ordinary folk, such as blacksmiths. 'Horses are the steeds of nobles, yet also the work aids of common folk in our history,' Dee Dee reminds me, and their endurance reflects our own throughout our shared history.

One theory is that the Obby Oss festival may have sprung from the same school of thought that worshipped the cult of Epona. Epona advocated that horses were messengers to the gods, travellers between worlds, transcending life, death, past and future. During the Obby Oss celebration, festival-goers sing of the Osses' birth, death and resurrection, the simplest and most beautiful lesson we can learn from the Earth itself. The cycle, the wheel, the seasons; however we acknowledge the rhythm of the year, we are drawn to these festivals and markers because they allow us to slow down and carefully observe a world that has become suffocatingly fast-paced. And as the wheel turns, always coming full circle, traditions rooted in the natural world are ones of comfort and consistency. It is unsurprising, then, that within this celebration, we have held on to the figure of the horse in our traditions, our artwork, our literature, our collective cultural heritage. A figure that has played a part in every act of the human story and will continue to do so, whether taking centre stage or hiding in the wings. Just as, night after night, Selene's divine chariot carries the moon across the sky, the horse will keep drawing our imaginations back and forth – on and on and on, for as long as we can hold a paintbrush or taste a pint of cider, or clasp a set of reins.

CHAPTER FOUR

Bread and Circuses

Once you start looking, it's impossible to unsee the clues left behind in everyday objects like pub, house and road names; clues that reveal a glimpse into a past world, a different way of living, and a different social structure entirely. One afternoon I was driving along a country lane in Sussex and saw so many horse-related names I had to google the area to see if it had a horsey history. The White Horse, Stable Cottage, Livery Corner, Stud Farm and Forge Lane are familiar names in every corner of the country because of how closely our lives were connected to horses.

Today, however, I wasn't looking for pubs or cottages. I was looking for a Roman road. Like all who watched *Horrible Histories* as a child, I think of Roman roads as long and straight, built for people to travel as quickly as they could, with as few bends as possible to reduce journey times and the risk of robbers lurking around corners. You can see exactly what a Roman road looks like from above by searching aerial shots of Ermine Street, Stane Street and Fosse Way, all of which run in a straight line for miles across England. The road I was currently on, however, was not straight in the slightest. It had been winding beneath oak trees and green banks coated in January frost for so long that I had almost declared myself lost when all of a sudden, I turned a corner and emerged onto an open stretch of road, long and straight as an arrow.

This must be the place – a quiet road in the middle of nowhere that would have once been a busy Roman travelling route. You would never know it had ever been anything but a sleepy country lane. Driving along it now, I still wouldn't have guessed its secrets if I hadn't been looking at it on Google Maps earlier that day. Nobody might have known if someone hadn't been analysing aerial shots of the area in 1949. When the Second World War ended, the Royal Air Force photographed almost all of the United Kingdom as part of a National Air Survey to help revise maps and assist with highways and planning work. The images are still used today to research how the landscape has shifted over time, although Google Maps has provided a more up-to-date service for the general public to use. It was this that I used to zoom in on the villages of Iping and Milland in Sussex, examining the quiet country road that ran between the two until – at last! I found what I was looking for.

Historians believe this route is one of the only surviving sections of a Roman road that was not only forgotten for centuries but almost lost altogether. It forms part of the Chichester to Silchester Way, a 40-mile route connecting two settlements that were once important regional capitals in Roman Britain. Only four miles of the original 40 remain in use today, including the stretch of road on which I was now parked. I stepped out, looked around and spotted the footpath that would take me closest to what I had come here to see: the site of the Iping Roman Posting Station – or, to give it its Latin name, the *mansio* of Iping Road.

The name *mansio* comes from *manere*, which means to stay. It was used to describe an official stopping place along a Roman road maintained by the central government for the use of its officials. Archaeologists believe this two-acre site on the Iping Road would have supported forces passing through with supplies and services, possibly including stables, wheelwrights, veterinarians and a blacksmith for the care of the horses. Posting stations like these were usually spaced at regular lengths along Roman roads, and roughly every four miles (the furthest a horse could be ridden at full speed), there would also be smaller stations called *mutationes*, where travellers could change horses and take refreshment on a smaller scale. On the continent, this system of *mutationes* allowed the emperor Tiberius to travel 400 miles from Germany to Milan to see his dying brother, who had himself been thrown from a horse. Tiberius rode day and night to reach him, using the stopping stations to change to a fresh horse; he arrived just in time to see his brother alive before returning to Rome with the body, escorting it on foot the whole way.

With the help of Wikipedia and a few archaeology blogs, I had found the site of the station. But what now lay before me? An ancient horseshoe in the dirt, a crumbling wall and a rusty coin or two? Not quite. It was an earthwork – the name archaeologists gave to artificial changes in land level made from piles of rocks and soil. Ancient people built them for many reasons, including as foundations for buildings or to enclose a space. What I was looking at was essentially a big pile of soil – a rectangular shape with rounded corners measuring 86m by 112m, running in a smooth, mounded line around a field. It wasn't quite as remarkable as the Watling Street station in modern-day Lichfield, whose remains of an inn and public baths are still visible above ground. Yet, there was still something incredible in seeing such an ancient landmark. This *mansio* was now a protected monument. It had not been fully excavated, but surface discoveries of Roman material had been made within the confines of the mound, and I couldn't help wondering what treasures still slept in the earth before me, hidden between the primrose leaves and oak roots and rabbit holes; echoes of everyday life, utterly mundane to their original owners but invaluable to us now.

I watched the *mansio* turn orange and brown in the setting sun. A flock of redwings flew close over my head and landed in the row of fruit trees that lined the footpath. It was difficult to imagine a huge Roman tavern here, complete with galloping horses and merrymaking soldiers, but I have often felt a presence in the slow and quiet lanes of Sussex, something old and mystical. Perhaps the author H. G. Wells felt the same when he used Iping as the setting for *The Invisible Man*, his 1897 novel about a man who invents a way to change the body's refractive index, so it neither absorbs nor reflects light. His failure to reverse it leads to theft, violence and murder, all staged around a quiet inn in Iping called the Coach and Horses. This inn seems to have been fictional, and the description of the village appears to match nearby South Harting rather than Iping. Even so, it was still easy to imagine the stranger arriving in this sleepy place, enveloped in the cloak of midwinter:

> The stranger came early in February, one wintry day, through a biting wind and a driving snow, the last snowfall of the year, over the down, walking from Bramblehurst railway station, and carrying a little black portmanteau in his thickly gloved hand. He was wrapped up from head to foot, and the brim of his soft felt hat hid every inch of his face but the shiny tip of his nose; the snow had piled itself against his shoulders and chest, and added a white crest to the burden he carried. He staggered into the Coach and Horses more dead than alive, and flung his portmanteau down. 'A fire,' he cried, 'in the name of human charity! A room and a fire!' He stamped and shook the snow from off himself in the bar, and followed Mrs. Hall into her guest parlour to strike his bargain. And with that much introduction, that and a couple of sovereigns flung upon the table, he took up his quarters in the inn.

I left the *mansio* and drove home beneath a peach sky, through twisting lanes of gnarled trees, the earth covered in frost where the sun was too weak to warm it. I wondered how many travellers had roamed these roads and how differently they had snaked across the map a century, five centuries, a thousand years ago. How had an entire road been lost? At what point did the *mansio* close, crumble and disappear from living memory? The earth gives, and the earth takes away.

I wove through the old trees and hedgerows with the window open to the cold air, and as the darkness drew in, I saw Venus appear in the sky. The only planet named after a female deity, the Roman goddess of love and beauty, she is the brightest object in the sky after the moon and the sun, her glow magnified by the thick sulphur clouds that swirl around her, reflecting the sun's light like a mirror. Who else had seen her shining through the old Sussex lanes? A Roman soldier or a traveller, or the horses that carried them back and forth beneath the trees. Whoever they were, their stories had since fallen to the keepers of the damp and dark — guarded forever by oak roots and rabbit runs.

U

If a Roman soldier left the Iping station one morning and galloped down to the city of Chichester, he and his horse would have found another main road leading back out of it, heading north-east towards London Bridge. This was Stane Street, a 57-mile-long road cutting straight through the South Downs, Greensand Ridge and North Downs of the south-east corner of England. Today, you can trace most of it by following the local A-roads, although the Surrey stretch of the route has been largely abandoned and is mostly made up of bridlepaths and earthworks, with *mansiones* and *mutationes* scattered along the way. On reaching London, the soldier could have joined another road that has since been buried, the discovery of which was only made by excavations in 1845. This was the road that carried Boudicca to London on her journey to fight the Romans and connected the capital with what is considered Britain's oldest recorded town. The road led to Camulodunum in Essex, which today is the town of Colchester.

Colchester has long been known for its Roman origins, but it wasn't until 2004 that the Colchester Archaeological Trust unearthed a unique building. Through their excavations, they discovered that a Roman circus had been built just outside the town wall in the early second century AD. Long abandoned after going out of use, the remains had been buried beneath an old garrison built in 1862 and were only rediscovered when workers dug a trench for electric cables to provide lighting for a nearby football match.

In the Roman Empire, the circus was a large open-air track used mainly for horse and chariot races, animal hunts and gladiatorial combat of the Russell Crowe kind. Despite its name (meaning 'circle'), the venue was usually shaped like an oval or rectangle, with a strip in the middle called a *spina*, decorated with columns, statues and obelisks. A rising ring of seats surrounding the central arena was built along three sides of the circus, with the fourth side holding the starting gates or *carceres*. From these gates, on the signal of the presiding magistrate, a storm of horse-drawn chariots flew onto the track and hurled themselves around seven laps of the circus until the fastest one reached the finish line to be declared the victor.

A traditional Roman chariot was pulled by four horses, known as a *quadriga*, an example of which can be seen atop the Wellington Arch in Hyde Park, London. The Arch was originally built as an entrance to Buckingham Palace but became a victory arch to celebrate Wellington's defeat of Napoleon. It is crowned by the largest bronze sculpture in Europe, depicting the Angel of Peace descending on the *quadriga* of war. Roman chariots were designed so that the inside horse, known as the *funalis*, was the strongest to set the pace and take the sharpest turns during a race. The *funalis* was also the most vulnerable to broken bones, strains, concussions and death, so it was often the only one named in celebratory inscriptions. The horses were bred with careful attention to conformation and pedigree, with the best stock coming from stud farms in North Africa and Spain, transported using specially designed ships called *hippago*.

The charioteers driving the horses were of a quite different background to their animal counterparts, usually slaves or freedmen of low social status. Races were so chaotic and dangerous that the charioteer had to carry a curved knife in the *fasciae* (protective bands) wrapped around his torso to cut himself out of tangled reins. Even if he managed to win a race, it was not always positive. On the continent, one Roman historian recorded how charioteers had been persecuted for witchcraft if they enjoyed too much success. Some even burned at the stake for their perceived crimes. For the more popular victors, however, the prize money could reach up to 60,000 sesterces for a single race, which would have paid for around 200 amphoras of wine. At the time, the poet Juvenal mourned that a chariot driver could earn a hundred times as much as a lawyer; it was Juvenal who famously coined the term 'bread and circuses' to refer to people being pacified by their government with food and entertainment. The writer and philosopher Dio Chrysostom described them as:

> ... a people to whom one need only throw bread and give a spectacle of horses since they have no interest in anything else. When they enter a theatre or stadium they lose all consciousness of their former state and are not ashamed to say or do anything that occurs to them ... constantly leaping and raving and beating one another and using abominable language and often reviling even the gods themselves and flinging their clothing at the charioteers and sometimes even departing naked from the show.

It's impossible to ignore the similarities with our modern-day view of football hooligans, who can encapsulate, all at once, the best and worst elements of competitive sport. There is nothing new in the human zeal for races, teams, winners and losers. It seems inevitable that once horses had been domesticated and put to work, their role would expand into recreation. Strong, fast, controllable but unpredictable, who better than the horse to excite the thrill-seekers, fortune-makers, gamblers, peasants and noblemen in the crowds? Just like our football stadiums and cricket pitches today, spaces in the landscape were marked out, built up and dedicated to sport and its spectators. And it wasn't just chariot races that made their mark; the Romans developed another equestrian sport that was so popular and lucrative for those involved that it has long become a permanent part of England's cultural identity.

$$\cup$$

Colchester's circus may have been buried and forgotten for centuries, but around 200 miles further north, in the city of York, one famous pastime is also thought to boast Roman roots. Historians have traced York's earliest equine sport as far back as 208AD when the Emperor Septimius Severus arrived from Rome to quell disorder in the region. To entertain and appease his troops at the garrison, Severus brought some Arabian horses and arranged for the staging of races on a stretch of land beyond the city walls. This area became known as Knavesmire, named after the mire and stream that had formed there naturally and which needed plenty of levelling and draining to be made into the horseshoe-shaped track it would eventually become. It was also an ancient area of common land, used by locals to graze their horses and livestock, which, during race days, would be driven to nearby Hob Moor to keep out of the way. Today, York Racecourse attracts around 360,000 racegoers per year, who come to watch, analyse and bet on the horses and their jockeys speeding around the track.[3]

Over the centuries, racing became a more established event at York Racecourse. Records show that the city

---

[3] It is also very close to the former Terry's Chocolate Works, the factory responsible for blessing the world with chocolate oranges. You can see the Grade II-listed art deco clock tower, with 'TERRY YORK' written on the face, from the tallest spectator boxes on the racecourse.

authorities officially supported it by 1530. In 1607, the year of the 'big freeze', races even took place on the frozen River Ouse between Micklegate Tower and Skeldergate Postern. In his history of York (titled *Eboracum* after the city's Roman name), Francis Drake recounted his experience of the freeze:

> About Martinmass began an extream frost; the river Ouze was wholly frozen up, so hard that you might have passed with cart and carriage as well as upon firm ground. Many sports were practised on the ice ... bowling, playing at football, cudgels ... and a horse-race was run from the tower at S. Mary-gate-end, along and under the great arch of the bridge, to the Crain at Skeldergate postern.

Frost fairs like these were a popular celebration in England between the seventeenth and early nineteenth centuries, when a period known as the Little Ice Age caused lower-than-average temperatures in the North Atlantic region. The River Thames frost fairs were well known further south in London, held on the tideway of the Thames. Witnesses recorded all kinds of activities taking place on the surface of the river, including horse and coach racing, fox hunting, bull baiting, an elephant parade, ice skating, bowling, archery and, on one December day in 1683, the roasting of a whole ox near Whitehall, part of which was eaten by King Charles II. The last London frost fair took place in 1814, after which the warming climate and restructuring of the River Thames' banks and bridges made it less and less likely to freeze and more likely to drown those who dared to step on the ice.

During the coldest years, the freezing of the water also saw a temporary end to one of the oldest forms of transport in the river's history, which disappeared entirely when Lambeth Bridge was built in 1862. Today, the only reminder of its existence is Horseferry Road in Westminster, named after an ancient ferry crossing that provided safe passage for

horses and carts needing to travel across the river. Before
1750, the only bridge crossing the Thames in the heart of
the city was London Bridge, which meant horse ferries
were a vital service for anyone wishing to cross. Both the
horses and carts were carried on a large raft-type vessel,
wide enough for both to fit and long enough to allow the
horses to stand in front of the cart without being taken out
of their harnesses. The most famous and well-used ferry was
found at Lambeth, crossing from St Mary's Church on the
east shore to Westminster on the west. At the time, the
Thames watermen were such an authority on the river that
when the proposal for building a bridge between the two
shores was first made, it was dropped due to opposition
from those who relied on the ferry for a living. With the
inevitable opening of the Lambeth Bridge, use of the ferry
declined, and the service finally closed – although it was
preserved, at least, in a street name.

Not all equestrian sports stood the test of time, like horse
racing. But there is another still practised sport – albeit not
taken seriously enough to be broadcast on TV or speculated
on by the bookmakers – that continues to capture our
imaginations centuries after it was first popularised in the
Middle Ages. Considered by some as Britain's first extreme
sport, its roots are deeply buried in the feudal system, land
ownership and the training of knights for battle. It became
so popular that within a hundred years of the first tournament
being recorded in 1066, a series of regulations were brought
in to limit them in case a real conflict arose, and the knights
were too busy competing. The sport was known as jousting,
its name taken from the Old French *joster*, meaning 'to
approach or meet'. The aim of the game was for two
mounted opponents to ride towards each other at high
speed, both wielding lances with blunted tips, and to strike

so hard at their opponent's armour that the lance would break or – even better – their opponent would be unhorsed.

The original purpose of jousting was a form of weapons training for soldiers on horseback; it coincided with the rise of heavy cavalry, a type of soldier mounted on powerful warhorses, who wore body armour and were armed with lances, swords, maces, axes and hammers. After William of Normandy's conquest in 1066, he devised a system to maintain control over England and gain loyalty (by force or favour) over the people whose former king he had defeated. Under his new feudal system, the king was the only absolute 'owner' of land, and any noblemen, knights or other tenants who wanted to manage it were granted the freehold in exchange for an oath of loyalty, the collection of local taxes on his behalf and the provision of local soldiers if they were needed. These soldiers were known as knights, and jousting (as well as archery and sword fighting) allowed them to develop skills in horsemanship and marksmanship while keeping fit between battles and providing entertainment for their fellow patriots. To enter the tournament, landowners would apply for a royal permit and choose their best knights to fight; in some cases, jousters who were not committed to a particular master could lend themselves out to the highest bidder, a form of temporary employment that became known as 'freelancing'.

As the decades passed, the Church officially condemned jousting tournaments as 'inventions of the devil', tempting the knights from the more 'noble' act of crusading. As a result, if a knight was killed during a tournament, they were forbidden burial on holy ground. Despite this, it continued to be a popular and lucrative sport for competitors and spectators. As the twelfth-century chronicler Roger of Howden wrote, it was encouraged as good training for the battlefield:

> A youth must have seen his blood flow, felt his teeth crack under his adversary's blows and been thrown to the ground twenty times … only then will he be able to face real war.

King Henry II eventually banned the tournaments to avoid
the violence and feuds they stoked, although his son Richard
the Lionheart brought them back under strict conditions.
When Henry VIII took the throne in 1509, he was known
for his love of hunting, jousting and tennis, but one infamous
accident may have altered the rest of his life and even
changed the course of history. The 44-year-old king fell
during a tournament and found himself trapped beneath his
horse. His injuries plagued him for the rest of his life, with
some believing the accident transformed him slowly from
the healthy, handsome man of his youth into the angry and
tyrannical leader he became. The accident likely caused his
ulcerated leg as well as brain injuries, and to make matters
worse, when the royal doctors were unable to heal the
damage, they discouraged him from taking part in too much
sport. That caused him to gain so much weight that,
according to one court visitor, 'three of the biggest men that
could be found could get inside his doublet.' In 2020,
researchers claimed to have located the jousting yard where
the accident happened, lost when Charles II demolished the
royal court; it is thought to be on the grounds of the National
Maritime Museum in Greenwich, which was once the
king's palace and favourite residence. Ground-penetrating
radar was used to scan the area, upon which the team found
traces of two octagonal towers, believed to be the remnants
of spectator stands.

The knights may have enjoyed the glory of the joust, but
they relied, of course, on the skill and courage of their horse
just as much as their own abilities. The rarest and most highly
prized type of horse was known as a *destrier*, highly intelligent
and trained specifically for battles and tournaments. They
were no bigger or smaller than regular riding horses of the
period, but their strong hind legs allowed them to shift their
weight and move quickly, meaning they could sprint, stop
and turn around with perfect ease and speed, as well as being
able to bite and kick on command. As the destrier was valued

at seven or eight times the cost of a regular horse, most knights rode other types of warhorse, such as coursers, which were light, fast and strong, or rounceys, an ordinary, all-purpose horse. All horses wore caparisons, an ornamental cloth decorated with the knight's coat of arms, and had their heads protected by an iron chanfron.

Competitive jousting declined when firearms and muskets arrived on the scene in the sixteenth century. It became a source of theatrical entertainment for the courts, before disappearing completely by the mid-seventeenth century. But although it fell out of favour as a serious sport, the image of the knight on horseback has become firmly imprinted in our national memory. The Age of Chivalry arose from the idealisation of the cavalryman; the word originates from the Old French term *chevalerie*, which means 'horse soldiery'. Initially only referring to the mounted military figure, the idea of chivalry evolved to include the Christian institution of knights fighting in the Holy Land and the fantasy of romance and courtly love. The chivalric code, popularised in legends like King Arthur and his knights of the Round Table, encouraged humility, courage, justice, discipline and faith, among other traits. Historians tend to agree, however, that although we associate chivalry with the 'golden' age of medieval England, it is unlikely to represent the past accurately. The Swiss historian Jean Charles Léonard de Sismondi referred to this when he wrote how the Age of Chivalry always seems to be further back than historians can verifiably pinpoint:

> The more closely we look into history, the more clearly shall we perceive that the system of chivalry is an invention almost entirely poetical ... It is always represented as distant from us both in time and place; and whilst the contemporary historians give us a clear, detailed, and complete account of the vices of the court ... of the ferocity or corruption of the nobles, and of the servility of the people, we are astonished

to find the poets, after a long lapse of time, adorning the very same ages with the most splendid fictions of grace, virtue and loyalty.

Despite its doubtful origin, the trope of the knight in shining armour still charms us hundreds of years later. One of my favourite films growing up was *A Knight's Tale*. It is loosely based on Chaucer's story of the same name, which follows a peasant squire called William Thatcher (played by the late, lovely Heath Ledger) as he poses as a knight to compete in tournaments and win the heart of a noble lady. On the more highbrow end of the spectrum, the character of the wandering, adventure-seeking knight has inspired poetry and fiction across the centuries, from the fourteenth-century Middle English romance *Sir Gawain and the Green Knight* to Edmund Spenser's epic poem *The Faerie Queene* and the parody novel *Don Quixote* by Miguel de Cervantes.

While most knights are now restricted to the screen or written page, the sport of jousting is still enjoyed worldwide – although only in a handful of locations. In England, spectators can enjoy annual jousting matches at Hever Castle in Kent (the childhood home of Anne Boleyn), Stonor Park in Oxfordshire and Warwick Castle in Warwickshire. Warwick is particularly suited to the sport, as it was historically the centre of tournaments, feasts and everything we might associate with the knight in shining armour. First built in 1068 by William the Conqueror, for centuries, it was inhabited by the de Beauchamp family, who were famous for their skills as jousters, sword-bearers and archers. Modern jousting now takes place on a safer scale with more consideration for the welfare of the horses, but it has not lost any of its pageantry or excitement.

Liam Bartlett, Operations Director at Warwick Castle, believes the charm of modern jousting is rooted in the fact that we only tend to see it on screen and rarely, if ever, in real life. 'Jousting,' he says, 'represents such a raw and brutal

symbol of resolution to conflict. This is paired with the
reality that jousting and "knights in shining armour" are
mainly represented in heroic and timeless movies and dramas,
and so many of us will never have witnessed this type of
thing in real life. It is this scarcity that drives such an incredible
sense of intrigue and fascination.' The jousting at Warwick is
also used to educate the visitors on a complex period of
England's history, the War of the Roses. As part of the joust,
the audience chooses a side to support in the decades-long
civil war: 'They join in on the action, supporting their
"household" as the iconic characters from each side do battle.
Each of these jousting battles represents a different stage of
the conflict, right through to the resolution and the formation
of House of Tudor.' Through the power of thundering
horses and towering knights, history is brought right back to
life. 'Using the simplicity of a joust helps break down a
complex and intricate period of history,' explains Liam. 'It
also stirs the imagination of our younger visitors in order
for them to engage with our history.'

But alas! Not all jousting arenas (or 'tilting rings') managed
to survive the turbulence of twenty-first-century life. In
Lancashire, England, just north of Liverpool, one former
ring is now only visible through the magic of Google Maps.
Closed off to the public since 2012, the Camelot Theme
Park was once a pseudo-medieval haven of Arthurian
legend, magic shows, falconry, rollercoasters and jousting.
Now abandoned after visitor numbers declined, a YouTube
video (see References, page 247) shows a drone passing over
dismembered mannequins, vandalised buildings, and a bleak,
rusty rollercoaster called the Knightmare. The jousting
arena, once decorated with bright colours and crests,
spectator stands and even a royal box for the king, now
stands deserted, the cheer of the crowds and the thump of
galloping hooves lost to history forever. At the time of
writing, the latest images on Google Maps show barely any
remains of the theme park, except for the iconic white and

teal castle entrance, slowly falling apart against a backdrop of copper and gold late autumn leaves. Despite the deterioration, the park looks almost peaceful without the crowds and ice cream stands. Nature, as she always does, has started to claim Camelot back for herself.

U

Two hundred miles south of where the Camelot jousting ring is returning to the earth (or being made into houses – its future is uncertain), another equestrian sport is far from disappearing. The rules of this once 'ruleless' game were first published at the Hurlingham in 1875, a private club set within 42 acres of grounds on the River Thames, where its first game of polo had been played the year before. The Hurlingham Polo Association has since become the governing body for polo in the United Kingdom, Ireland and 36 other countries, despite the game itself originating as far from London as is possible to imagine. First played over 2,500 years ago by the nomadic tribesmen of Central Asia, the game was originally used to hone horsemanship and combat skills, migrating over the centuries from Persia to Arabia, Tibet, India, China and Japan. The name is thought to be an Anglicisation of the Tibetan Balti word for 'ball'.

As both an equestrian and a spectator, my experience of polo is limited. Unless it's a game of Articulate or Bananagrams, I'm not a competitive person, and I find it difficult to get emotionally invested in sports matches of any kind. I am also not someone who enjoys speed; when I was learning to drive, I asked my instructor whether I could just travel everywhere in first gear, a request he sadly refused. However, as an undergraduate in Bristol, I once spent a whole day attempting polo. At the time, I was a member of my university's riding club, mainly to exploit the subsidised cost of lessons but also to escape the city now and then; to breathe sweet air on horseback in the leafy hills of the Mendips, riding across sunlit slopes scattered with rocks and gorges. One term, we were invited by the university polo team to try playing polo. I'm not sure if they were looking for more players or just being kind, but by the end of the day (spoiler alert!), none of us had been invited to join the team.

For someone accustomed to plodding along on a big, lazy hacking horse, hopping on to a polo pony was quite a contrast, akin to switching from a transit van to a go-kart. The gentlest nudge of my heels would send the pony shooting forward at full speed, while the slightest pull of the reins would cause it to swerve around and canter off in the other direction before I knew what was happening. I had just gotten used to the motion without falling off when they gave me a mallet to hold, complete with a cigar-shaped head on the end. I was somehow supposed to canter along, one-handed, on my peppy little pony, then reach over with the mallet and whack a ball on the ground as I rode past, all while keeping an eye on the rest of the players and having some game strategy in my head. Reader, I hit not one single ball. I can't say it wasn't fun because once I adapted to the change of pace, there was plenty to enjoy in the thrill of it all and the team atmosphere. But it was my one and only experience of polo, and I have no plans to repeat it any time soon.

There are now many polo clubs established across the UK, including Cowdray Park in Midhurst, five miles from the Roman *mansio* I visited in Iping. The sport's exotic origins meant that it wasn't until the height of the Empire in the 1850s that polo became part of British culture. A group of tea planters is said to have discovered the sport in Manipur on the border with Burma (modern-day Myanmar) and founded the first club in nearby Assam. Other clubs were set up in Calcutta and Malta by British officers stopping off on their way home from India. In 1869, a British cavalry captain read about the game in *The Field* magazine and organised the first ever match in England, after which the sport became increasingly popular. In the 150 years since it was first played in the UK, the aim of the game has remained much the same. Two opposing teams of four riders play against each other on horseback, using a wooden mallet to hit a hard ball through the other team's goal; when a goal is scored, the teams switch ends, a rule that dates back to when the game was played in India, and the low sun was considered a disadvantage to one team. The game lasts one to two hours and is divided into several short periods called chukkas, which last around seven minutes. The mounts are known informally as polo ponies and are bred for their quick bursts of speed, stamina and agility, and for being responsive under pressure and not easily spooked. They are trained to be ridden one-handed, responding to the rider's leg and shifting weight to signal them to move forward, turn around and stop.

Since the first game was played at Hurlingham in 1874, the grounds have also gained croquet and tennis lawns, botanical gardens and a Georgian clubhouse. Like the game of polo that has become so intertwined with the club's identity, it is, undoubtedly, a place designed for a particular cross-section of society. Membership waiting lists that were once 30 years have now closed entirely due to the high demand. And according to rumour, when the billionaire oligarch Roman Abramovich tried to buy the club, he was immediately refused, even when he offered to pay each member £1 million as part of the deal.

Despite its wealth, polo is no longer regularly played at the club after the size of its grounds was significantly reduced after the war; the polo fields were purchased by Hammersmith and Fulham Council and used to build affordable housing. The club still stands in the same place it has occupied for over 150 years, but as with so many spaces in London, the wealthiest communities often live just a stone's throw from the poorest. The estate built on the polo fields is certainly not one of the most poverty-stricken in the city. However, it still endures its share of violence, anti-social behaviour, theft and vandalism that often accompanies life below the poverty line. And when just around the corner lie the beautiful gates and pristine lawns of Hurlingham, you can't help but find the contrast jarring.

Equestrian sports are often associated with the more elite social classes, none more so than polo. But tracing the game back to its roots reveals that polo was once a sport for everyone, played by anyone who could get their hands on the village pony – less Veuve Clicquot and more 'jumpers for goalposts'. It is wonderful to see such an old game still embraced with so much enthusiasm, to watch the players ride so elegantly across the field, their horses alive with energy and the crowds soaking up the sun. Clubs like Hurlingham, Cowdray, Beaufort and Cirencester offer picture-perfect views of the English countryside, the finest landscape gardening on show and a decent selection at the bar. It is nobody's fault that these spaces have become so exclusive – and many would argue that this is part of their charm. But in my experience, the most beautiful things in life are better shared, and you can't hear that ethereal chime of a champagne glass if there is nobody to toast with. The luxuries of a polo club may never lose their appeal, the horses never lose their shine, and the jodhpurs never lose their bleachy pristineness. Sport brings us together when the more serious aspects of life drive us apart, and there will never not be someone willing to invest in a club or sponsor a game. But it would be lovely if just a little of that money could be rerouted to those who need it most. Perhaps the philosopher Francis Bacon put it best when he observed: 'money is like muck, not good except that it be spread.'

CHAPTER FIVE

The Highwayman

In the village of Sheet, just north-east of Petersfield, Hampshire, a large horse chestnut tree grows on the village green. It was planted there in 1897 to commemorate Queen Victoria's Diamond Jubilee, and from the garden of the Queen's Head pub, home to, in my opinion, the finest pint of cider in all the land, you can see the thick, green branches shooting up into the summer sky, shading all who choose to stop and rest beneath them. There is a photograph online taken one year after it was planted. The tree is tiny and almost unnoticeable, enclosed in a protective metal gate, and behind it, a white horse and cart stand beside a row of stone cottages, one of which is the blacksmith's forge. This forge is now a residential cottage and no longer in commercial use, but its location is so symbolic of nineteenth-century rural life you could gaze at the closed door and still imagine the blacksmith working today – a horse waiting patiently by the wall, the *tink tink* of hammered metal and smoke rising from the chimney.

This quiet village was once a popular stop on one of the great coaching roads of the nineteenth century. In the warm summer months of the late 1830s – the heyday of coaching before the railways arrived – around 1,200 people would have passed through each week. The A3 still runs from London to Portsmouth, but a bypass was built in 1992, the year I was born, that skirted around Petersfield, Liphook and the villages in between. Before this, the road ran through the town of Petersfield, and on their way in or out of the town, horse-drawn travellers might have stopped in Sheet to visit the blacksmith whose forge still stands today. Traditional forges like these were often found in the centre of the village, usually near a crossroads and with space outside for horses and vehicles to wait, with a drinking trough and loops on the walls for tethering the animals. Chestnut trees like the one in Sheet also became symbolic of the village smithy, grown for the shade they cast on warm, sunny days; as for their horsey name, it is said to originate from when they were first introduced here from Turkey in the late sixteenth century. When the leaves fall, the stalk breaks away, revealing a scar on the twig that looks a little like a horseshoe – complete with nail holes. When crushed, they were also thought to relieve horses of coughs before modern veterinary medicines were developed.

Like many small villages in England, Sheet was once a hub of rural trade and craft, commemorated by a sign commissioned by the local community in the 1970s. Chichester-based artist Harold Thompson painted a fleece for the wool industry, two gold horns to symbolise the coaching road, and a waterwheel for the nearby mills that carried water from the Ashford stream and fuelled industries in tanning and ironwork. Local blacksmith Steven Pibworth then forged the sign's frame, and it now stands on the village green beside the chestnut tree – a nod to the past, created in the present.

It is easy to wander through quiet villages and imagine they have always been peaceful. They have become sanctuaries from the noise and intensity of modern life, all cobbled paths and timber beams, pub lunches and Women's Institute meetings. Today these villages are highly valued, sought-after places to live, especially by those from a more affluent background. But not so long ago, they were home to everyday people from above and below the poverty line, craftspeople who made horseshoes, spun wool and traded with travellers who stopped on their way along the Portsmouth road. When paths and tracks wove through the country like serpents, rising and falling along the contours of the land. When we moved by hoof, wheel or foot along the dark road, always at the mercy of nature – and each other. What stories of light and darkness can these old roads tell us? And what remains of the travellers who used them?

U

It was the last week of November, so I played Christmas tunes to Olive and the dogs as we drove north-east towards the Surrey Hills. The trees that lined the dual carriageway were still beautiful in their late autumn shades, but the golds had turned to browns and the browns to mulch; the darkness of winter had started to creep quietly in. We turned off before the Hindhead Tunnel and, after a few minutes, drove into the National Trust car park perched on the edge of the Devil's Punch Bowl, a 700-acre horseshoe-shaped valley covered in heather and crowned with woodland. Today was a cold day, and a pool of mist had formed in the dark heart of the Punch Bowl through which the sun could not penetrate. I could hear a wren singing at the car park edge and dogs barking happily in the distance. Olive was packed into the pram with a blanket and hot water bottle, and our dogs were unclipped and released into the morning light that glowed blood red against the dying bracken. All was still and quiet.

The path we were following turned right under a birch tree and emerged at a crossroads. A long track stretched out far ahead to the edge of the Punch Bowl, and a sign and sculpture marked the point where we admired the view, standing at the heart of the clearing. The sign told the story of a road restored. On this spot, where the air was so peaceful and rabbits grazed beneath the scrub, the A3 road once ran for 200 years, with three lanes of traffic carrying thousands of cars and lorries from Portsmouth to London every day. It was almost impossible to imagine, except for the remnants that still lay hidden in the grass; a cat's eye, a piece of metal, a slice of orange plastic. Aside from these relics you would never know this was still a road less than two decades ago.

The history of this empty road was rooted in the dockyard at Portsmouth, around 30 miles south-west of the Punch Bowl. King Richard I ordered the first dock to be built there in 1194, creating a hub for the Royal Navy that would later help Britain become one of the most powerful and invasive countries in the world. Because of the dockyard's position, a decent road from London to Portsmouth was vital but the sandstone hills at Hindhead, halfway between the two cities, meant the road initially had to pass over the top. This required all travellers to climb, either on foot or horseback, up a notoriously long and steep hill, which was said to be bleak, lonely and exposed to all weathers. It consequently became a favourite haunt of the highwayman, the name given to a thief mounted on horseback who held travellers at gunpoint on the darkest, most isolated stretches of road. Once stopped, the victims would be robbed of their money, jewels and valuables before the highwayman remounted his horse and rode off into the night. If the victims were lucky and compliant, no bullets would be fired.

We began the climb along the upper ridge of the Punch Bowl, where the old road used to run before it was rebuilt further down in the 1830s. As we rose, the view widened out in a swathe of burnt colour, heather gone to seed, and gorse bushes dark and thorned. Corvids were soaring through the sky above us, and I could hear crows yelling and a magpie chattering back. A beautiful yet stark winter landscape, the summer flowers long since slipped away and the trees bare of their autumn softness. This would have been a haunting road on which to travel alone on a starless night. If I closed my eyes, I could almost hear galloping in the distance, the heaving of a horse in motion, the beating of hoof against sandy earth –

Tlot-tlot, in the frosty silence! *Tlot-tlot*, in the echoing night!

Could a poem more finely capture the horse's gait than Alfred Noyes' 'The Highwayman'? First published in 1906, it was written when the poet was staying in a cottage on the edge of Bagshot Heath, a large forest only 20 miles north of the Punch Bowl, once described by Daniel Defoe as 'a vast tract of land … given up to barrenness, horrid and frightful to look on.' (I value his opinion; he would later go on to accurately describe my hometown as one 'eminent for little but being full of good inns'.) When Alfred Noyes stayed at Bagshot Heath after leaving university, he agreed it was 'a wild bit of country', with the sound of the wind in the pine trees inspiring the famous first lines of the poem and the story that followed:

> The wind was a torrent of darkness among the gusty trees.
> The moon was a ghostly galleon tossed upon cloudy seas.
> The road was a ribbon of moonlight over the purple moor,
> And the highwayman came riding –
>   Riding – riding –
> The highwayman came riding, up to the old inn-door.

The poem is thought to be based on a true story, told to Noyes during his stay in an area rife with highwaymen lying in wait for passing stagecoaches, the desolate heathland landscape being the perfect spot for armed robbery. In the poem, a daring and handsome highwayman visits his lover Bess at her father's inn; a jealous ostler (the name given to the stableman employed at a coaching inn) overhears their plans to meet again and betrays them to the authorities. A troop of soldiers waits at the inn where the lovers have agreed to meet, binding and gagging Bess so she cannot warn him of the ambush. Knowing his return will lead to his death, she reaches for a musket and shoots herself in the chest, sacrificing herself so her highwayman lover might hear the shot and turn away from where the soldiers lie in wait. When he learns of her death, the highwayman is killed

when he returns to avenge her. The poem ends with the
two lovers meeting as ghosts on the darkest winter nights,
with the sound of 'the horsehoofs ringing clear':

> Over the cobbles he clatters and clangs in the dark inn-yard.
> He taps with his whip on the shutters, but all is locked and barred.
> He whistles a tune to the window, and who should be waiting
> there
> But the landlord's black-eyed daughter,
> > Bess, the landlord's daughter,
> Plaiting a dark red love-knot into her long black hair.

Love, loss and death — the perfect trio for a backdrop like
the Surrey heathland, wild in the winter sun and desolate in
the dark.[4] As we continued to climb the long track to the
top, we passed the Sailor's Stone, a headstone marking the
site of another gruesome murder from the eighteenth
century. Along this road, a sailor was killed by three men he
had befriended in the nearby Red Lion Inn on his way from
London to Portsmouth. With no money to buy food or
drink, the sailor bought them ale with a golden guinea he
had received from his last voyage, but after leaving, he was
set upon by the men, who cut his throat, and stole his
clothes and belongings; they were caught hours later at the
Sun Inn in Rake, trying to sell their loot. They were tried
and found guilty six months later and hanged on what is
now Gibbet Hill, just up the path from where a local squire
erected the headstone. The murderers' bodies were preserved
in tar and hung in irons for three years until a storm blew
them down, a stark warning to anyone tempted to commit
a crime on this eerie highway.

---

[4] For a fuzzy, straight-out-of-the-eighties visual depiction of the poem,
see the music video for Fleetwood Mac's *Everywhere*. For the cake-
inspired version, see Julia Donaldson's *The Highway Rat*.

Elsewhere in the country, highways up and down the land were plagued by robbers and murderers. Perhaps the most famous was the highwayman Dick Turpin, whose exploits were also turned into a poem by Alfred Noyes. Turpin has become more mythic, and most of the things we know about him are false. Accused of horse theft, murder and highway robbery, Turpin was famously said to have ridden his horse, Black Bess, from London to York in record time to provide himself with an alibi for a crime. Harrison Ainsworth immortalised his journey in his popular 1834 novel *Rookwood*, in which he described Turpin galloping north at midnight:

His blood spins through his veins; winds round his heart; mounts to his brain. Away! Away! He is wild with joy.

This romantic, Robin Hood-style version of Turpin has little basis in fact. Turpin began stealing at a young age before joining a gang in Essex, using his knowledge as an apprentice butcher to help poach cattle. He was also known to have robbed a farmhouse, throwing boiling water over the elderly owner, and for shooting his accomplices when their crimes were botched. He was so reviled that when he was finally hanged in 1739, on the famous Knavesmire racecourse in York, of all places, the only mourners at his execution were paid 10 shillings each to be there by Turpin himself. A witness described how Turpin 'went off this stage with as much intrepidity and unconcern as if he had been taking a horse to go on a journey'.

Fortunately, by the late eighteenth century, highway robbery had declined due to many changes to the roads, including the revocation of licences from taverns providing highwaymen with sanctuary, the decrease in isolated stretches of road due to urbanisation, and the development of banking, which meant people carried less money on the road. In 1749, a group of six men called the Bow Street

Horse Patrol, later known as the Bow Street Runners, was also established by John Fielding and his half-brother, the author Henry Fielding, who worked as a magistrate in Bow Street, London. The patrol was formed to combat the rise in highway robbery. Furnished with handcuffs, a pistol and a cutlass, the men were paid a guinea a week to catch criminals. It was so successful that highwaymen were almost eradicated and government funding for the project stopped, resulting in cases surging once again. By 1800, there were 68 Bow Street Runners back in operation, who continued to fight crime until they were eventually absorbed into the newly formed Metropolitan Police in 1829.

The wooden upright of the Punch Bowl's gibbet survived long after the last body was hung from it. It was seen by the artist J. M. W. Turner in the early nineteenth century, shortly before he produced his *Liber Studiorum*, a collection of prints created between 1807 and 1819. A number of these were titled 'Hind Head Hill' and varied between sketched, watercolour and copper plate versions of the same image, as seen by Turner from his stagecoach as he journeyed through the Surrey Hills. The mezzotint engraving from 1811 is perhaps the most striking; the gibbet is in full view atop the sweeping landscape and almost looks like it is ascending to heaven. To the right, as the lonely road disappears behind the hill, Turner has included a stagecoach like the one that would have carried him, jostled by the movement of the horse, as he sketched and wrote a few lines of verse in the back of his sketchbook:

Hind head thou cloud-capt winded hill
In every wind that heaven does fill

On thy dark heath the traveler mourns
Icey night approach & groans

The low wan sun has downward sunk
The steamy Vale looks dark and dank

The doubtful roads scarce seen
Nor sky lights give the doubtful green
But all seems drear & horror

Hark the kreaking irons
Hark the screeching owl

With the murder of the Unknown Sailor, the gibbet creaking in the wind, and the dark, desolate path plagued by highwaymen, it's no wonder this stretch of the London to Portsmouth road gained a reputation for being haunted. There were so many brutal murders along the route that the Portsmouth road became known as the Road of Assassination. In 1851, to dispel residents' fears, a local politician even erected a Celtic cross on Gibbet Hill, which remains in place today. But the road continued to be popular with highwaymen, who took advantage of the stagecoaches' slow ascent up the hill until it was finally moved in 1822 to a route further down into the Punch Bowl. The increase in wheeled traffic around the south-east had caused so much deterioration in the surface of the road that the government allowed companies called Turnpike Trusts to maintain them and charge tolls in exchange. The Portsmouth road was taken over by the Kingston-upon-Thames to Sheet Bridge Turnpike Company and was eventually rerouted to stop the horses becoming so exhausted as they heaved the carriages and stagecoaches behind them. The road's construction was also completed through human- and horsepower alone, with labourers moving tens of thousands of tons of soil by hand.

While, in theory, turnpikes helped to keep the roads smoother and safer, they were not always welcome. Many saw them as yet another way of squeezing more taxes from the common people, removing the rights of passage they had always been entitled to. Charges on the turnpike were also difficult to calculate, and the gatekeepers responsible for interpreting the regulations and collecting the tolls were often attacked and assaulted by those who refused to pay. Initial charges on one of Hampshire's local turnpikes included:

> For every horse One Penny; For every Stage or Coach drawn by four or more horses One Shilling; For every Coach drawn by one or two horses Sixpence; For every Waggon with four wheels drawn by five or more horses One Shilling; For every other Cart or Waggon Sixpence; For every score of oxen or cattle Ten Pence; For every score of sheep or lambs Five pence; For every score of hogs Five pence.

At the edge of the path, just along from the Gibbet Hill viewpoint, a milestone announces that Hyde Park Corner is 39 miles away, and Portsmouth is 30. These stone posts were compulsory on all turnpike roads, not only to guide travellers on their way, but also to help coaches keep to their schedule. This particular milestone was reinstated when the Hindhead Tunnel was built in 2010. It had fallen down the bank of the Punch Bowl, just off the route of the old A3, so the contractor hauled it out and gave it to the National Trust for safekeeping until the tunnel was complete. Using old Ordnance Survey maps and local knowledge, the Trust's archaeology team and the Milestone Society authenticated the milestone as an original feature from the old turnpike road, dating back to 1811, and found in almost the same position to which it has since been restored.

As most modern roads are now tarmacked, it is easy to forget that many local routes like the old Punch Bowl road were incredibly rough. The damage done by hundreds of horses' hooves traversing the lanes every day, pummelling into the ground, or etching grooves with the wheels of their carts, became an ongoing maintenance task often taken on by local labourers. Most of the time, these roads were built and repaired using locally sourced materials, so the hardness and durability of one road could differ hugely from another, depending on the geology of the area. On the other side of Petersfield, at the opposite end to Sheet, there is another village called Buriton, whose history is bound up in the chalk and lime industries that flourished thanks to the natural chalk pits quarried there for hundreds of years. The abundance of chalk and flint was used to maintain the busy village roads, with piles of broken flints kept nearby to fill the ruts. Farm workers collected flints from the fields during the quiet winter months and sold them to the council for road repair, measured by piling the flints into wooden frames with a handle at each end. Romani travellers were known to offer a day's work to break up the flints, raking and hammering until they were small enough to create a hard, solid surface. The rough flint was useful for horses travelling up and down the steep tracks of the South Downs, described by Charles Dickens as 'a height so steep as to be hardly accessible to any but the sheep and goats that fed upon its sides'. The creamy whiteness of the stones lit the path for those who travelled under moonlight, and the road became known locally as the Milky Way.

Like Sheet, Buriton was a thoroughfare of horse-drawn traffic before the bypass road was built, providing a welcome sanctuary for travellers moving through an often perilous area. The network of roads south of Petersfield was particularly treacherous, full of robbers and highwaymen who lurked in the leafy darkness of the Forest of Bere. In 1662, on travelling through the area, the diarist Samuel Pepys wrote that he had 'hired a countryman to guide us to Havant to avoid going through the forest'. Between Buriton and Clanfield, where the Queen Elizabeth Country Park now lies, an old coaching inn called Bottom Inn still stands as a residential cottage. In *Nicholas Nickleby*, Charles Dickens describes coming upon this inn beneath the twilight and asking the landlord about the road ahead to Portsmouth:

'Twelve miles,' said Nicholas, leaning with both hands on
his stick, and looking doubtfully at Smike.

'Twelve long miles,' repeated the landlord.

'Is it a good road?' inquired Nicholas.

'Very bad,' said the landlord. As of course, being a landlord,
he would say.

'I want to get on,' observed Nicholas, hesitating. 'I scarcely
know what to do.'

'Don't let me influence you,' rejoined the landlord. 'I
wouldn't go on if it was me.'

By the end of the eighteenth century, the improved turnpike
roads increased traffic so much that coaching inns and stables
could be found every few miles, with at least one inn
operating in every market town in England. During the
'golden age' of coaching (around the 1830s), an estimated
150,000 horses were in use, and in busy cities like London,
coaching inns acted as termini for passengers, welcoming
them after long journeys across town and country. Some of
the busiest inns were known to house as many as 1,800
horses to supply travellers – although facilities were often
basic, if not poor; in some stables, the stalls were only divided
by wooden planks suspended from the ceiling. As stagecoaches
could only travel for short 'stages' of around 10–15 miles, they
were required to stop frequently to change the horses and
give the travellers food and rest, although depending on the
price of their ticket, they may have found themselves sharing
a bed with a stranger. Compared to modern standards, the
early stagecoaches were also incredibly slow, travelling only
four to six miles an hour depending on the road surface and
weather conditions. But in 1754, a Manchester-based
company advertised a service called the 'flying coach', which
it claimed could travel at the blink-and-you'll-miss-it speed
of eight miles an hour, zooming from Manchester to London
in just four and a half days. But no matter the speed, travelling
by stagecoach for any length of time was never comfortable,

with poor suspension, bumpy roads, and the ever-lingering smell of unbathed humans, sweaty horses and manure.

Typically, a busy coaching inn was built around a central courtyard and set of stables, with a tall arched gate leading in and out from the open road. The courtyard would have been alive with activity all day and night; horns announcing the arrival of coaches at all hours, hooves clattering across the cobblestones, and the bustle of travellers arriving and departing. Needless to say, coaching inns weren't famous for a restful night's sleep. Just south of the River Thames in Southwark, a building known as the George Inn is thought to be the last remaining galleried inn in London, originally extending around three sides of a courtyard so the guests could keep an eye on things from their bedroom windows. Two-thirds of it was demolished some time ago to make way for the railway, but most of the building still stands, and it is now in the care of the National Trust; one bar even contains a rare tavern clock, whose large dials helped travellers and coach drivers set their watches as they passed through.

With the surge of the railways, demand for stagecoaches dwindled, and by the mid-nineteenth century, most London-based coaches had been withdrawn from service. And while some coaches were still used in the places railways hadn't yet reached, many of the coaching inns closed over time, with the rest adapting to become regular pubs or hotels, or converting the stables to garages. The roads continued to improve until the motor car became the new king of the highway, and the old rubble tracks and thoroughfares became smoother and slicker, rebuilt and rerouted through the landscape to avoid the steepest climbs and sharpest corners.

And yet, in the face of so many decades of motorisation, here I was in the heart of Surrey, walking down an old road that had not seen a stagecoach, let alone a motor car, for almost two centuries. It was almost impossible to imagine this place being anything other than a nature reserve – except, perhaps, if you looked at an aerial shot and saw how heavily the old roads were etched into the land. As I left the path that took me down from Gibbet Hill to the old A3 trunk road, I felt a marked change in the track. No more steep climbs or sharp twists beneath leafy canopies, echoes of the old route once travelled on foot, by stagecoach or by horse and rider. The new road was wide open and flat, exposed to the sky and with plenty of room for the cars that drove along here as recently as 2011, before this road, too, was closed. I would have been nine when I last travelled here in the back of my parents' car, but I can't remember it at all, even after watching dash-cam footage on YouTube. When it was finally opened to the public, the Hindhead Tunnel syphoned cars underground, returning the Punch Bowl to a sanctuary for both wildlife and people. In 10 short years, a place that was once clogged with traffic jams and air pollution was now almost silent except for the sound of buzzards mewing and a dog barking somewhere in the distance. Where there was once tarmacked road, a thin layer of earth now covered the ground; the contractors buried the old road using sandstone from the route of the newly dug tunnel. The area was being scraped and moulded back into the original contour of the hillside, as if the road had never existed at all.

The cars may have vanished underground but decades after the last stagecoach travelled through here, or the last person rode their horse from London to Portsmouth, there were still horses roaming through the deep, wooded heart of the Devil's Punch Bowl. Around 40 miles of bridleways and footpaths thread their way around the rim of the valley and over on to the heather-strewn mounds of nearby Hindhead Commons. The saddlebags of the eighteenth century have been replaced by high-vis jackets and body protectors, and a ride around the Punch Bowl is now a recreational pastime; a no-longer-harrowing commute along a formerly dark and murderous highway, more trotting and chatting with a cup of coffee to finish. And it isn't only the equestrian community that have brought horses back into the Punch Bowl. On quiet days, some visitors are lucky enough to stumble upon the elusive Exmoor ponies that graze this area all year round. Their presence is part of a National Trust project to restore and maintain the heathland, a habitat that has become globally rarer than rainforest. When commoners stopped grazing their livestock on the land after the war, it soon became overwhelmed by birch, pine and bracken, species that would eventually return the heath to forest if the ponies and cattle weren't here to reduce new growth.

I finished my walk and eyeballed a tea room with glee, before taking one final glance at the path beneath my feet and the bowl of heather blossom and wooded streams that sank down into the earth to my right. This magical place was said to be the largest spring-formed feature in the UK created by water cutting into the rocks, an erosive force that is still taking place today at the bottom of the valley. Once a haunted thoroughfare for travellers and their horses, coaches and carts, it is now a sanctuary for wildlife, including all three of our native woodpecker species, nightjars, Dartford warblers, cuckoos, dormice, bats, deer and rare species of wildflowers and insects. To wander here, day or night, felt like time travel. Below my feet I could see the shadows of an old road; pieces of plastic debris still hiding in the smooth, straight edges of the track that would take a little longer to be reshaped by new growth. Within the vast age of our ancient landscape, barely a second had passed since cars roared through here, and only a minute before that, the earth was still imprinted with horseshoes and cartwheels. Now there were only footprints in the dust, and the shoeless marks of ponies roaming from bracken to birch. Defined now by its absence of cars and coaches, it was still, in its way, a highway, ingrained into the land like all the others.

In the same way that our roads first evolved to carry horses and their passengers, another kind of highway was also invented with horsepower in mind. This highway, however, was a floating one – and it was called a canal. These channels may look similar to rivers and other waterways, but whereas rivers are naturally formed and shaped by the rain cycle, canals are designed and built by human hands. Their original purpose was to carry goods from one place to another, using the natural movement of water to speed things along. The Chinese are considered to be the pioneers of canals, building the Grand Canal of China in the tenth century to link up trade routes. But it was the Romans who brought canals to Britain, building the Fossdyke canal from Lincoln to the River Trent for drainage and navigation, as well as the Caer Dyke, the remains of which now form an 85-mile-long ditch along the western edge of the Fens on the east coast of England.

In the eighteenth century, a surge in canal building driven by the Industrial Revolution gave rise to what has since been called the Golden Age of canals. It began with the construction of the Bridgewater canal, which led from the Duke of Bridgewater's coal mines in Worsley right into the heart of Manchester. With the help of engineer James Brindley, the duke built it so that it connected to a series of tunnels leading into the mines, which meant the coal could simply be loaded up and immediately transported for sale. This resulted in cheaper deliveries, which halved the price of coal in Manchester overnight, and went on to inspire similar projects all over the country. The next 20 years saw the construction of some of the most important canals in the country, paid for by the merchants, aristocrats, bankers, textile manufacturers, pottery barons and mine owners who benefited from this innovative mode of transport. Some channels were less financially viable than others, but the overall surge helped Britain to become one of the first industrial superpowers in the world.

In the early days of the canal systems, before the invention of the steam engine, all boats and barges were towed along the water using a horse, mule, hinny, pony or sometimes a pair of donkeys.[5] Horses were such a vital part of the infrastructure that many of the original canal-side buildings were designed with horses in mind. In Birmingham, a purpose-built stable called the Roundhouse was completed on Sheepcote Street in the 1870s, originally designed to look after the horses and store goods for passing canal traffic. The design could house 49 horses overnight, and enabled horse-drawn carts to enter from the lower outer yard using a tunnel and ramp, where they could offload and reload stock. In King's Cross, the London Canal Museum stands on the site of an old Victorian ice warehouse once owned by the Swiss ice cream entrepreneur Carlo Gatti. Ice was shipped all the way from Norway to London and carried along the canal by horse-drawn barge, where it was then stored in the ice wells underneath the building and made into ice cream for those who could afford the luxury. Horses were such an integral part of Gatti's business model, the building had specially designed ramps, stables and even accommodation for the stable keeper.

Elsewhere, along the slow and steady towpaths of Britain, a number of different stable buildings were built to house travellers, tradesmen and their horses. In Llanymynech, Powys, the Montgomery Canal was used to carry quarried limestone; today, a visitor centre now open to the community is based in the stables of the old Sun Inn, and surrounded by the remains of tramways, kilns and other echoes of Wales' industrial past. On the Thames and Severn Canal, examples of lengthsmen's cottages from the 1790s can still be found in

---

[5] 'Mule' and 'hinny' are names for the offspring of a horse and a donkey. The mule is sired by a male donkey and a female horse, whereas a hinny is sired by a female donkey and a male horse. Most mules and hinnies are sterile.

Chalford, Coates, Cerney Wick, Marston Meysey and Inglesham. Lengthsmen were employed to maintain locks and care for towpaths along English canals; their cottages, built with stone and a plaster or stucco finish, were cylindrical and stacked over three floors, the lowest of which was used as a stable for the horses. Others were attached to canal pubs and inns, like the cylindrical building still found at the Boat House pub in Daventry, Northamptonshire.

In their heyday, horse-drawn canal boats were a surprisingly efficient means of transport; at a steady walk, a canal horse could pull 50 times as much cargo in a boat than it could in a cart or wagon, especially when the water helped it to avoid the roughest roads. But assisting the horse along the towpath was a skill in itself, and a number of tips and tricks were required to pass along the canal. The earliest tunnels, for example, were not built with towpaths, as the boreholes would have needed to be so big the tunnels would not have been financially viable. So how could a barge move through a tunnel if it was tied to a horse on the bank? The answer was given to me by my mother-in-law Chris, who grew up near the city of Birmingham, home to one of the most intricate canal networks in the world. To move through the tunnel, two people would lie on their backs, on top of the boat or on specially designed planks jutting out from either side. Keeping their legs at a 45-degree angle and their feet on the tunnel roof, they would then 'walk' the boat along the tunnel in a motion known as 'legging' – this is where the expression 'legging it' comes from. As the boat moved through the tunnel, a third person would unhook the horses and lead them up over the hillside to the other end, reconnecting them when the boat finally reappeared. During the Industrial Revolution, legging it through a tunnel took such a long time it became an actual profession. The Standedge Tunnel beneath the Pennines, for example, was more than three miles long and could take up to three hours to get through, depending on the boat's weight.

A further problem to solve was moving your horse across the canal when there was only one towpath that suddenly changed sides. The answer lay in a purpose-built structure known as a roving bridge or turnover bridge, which had brick-studded ramps on either side to allow the horse to move across more easily. The ramps were even placed on the same side of the bridge so the towlines didn't need to be unhitched. Some of the most beautiful examples of these stone bridges can still be found today on the Macclesfield Canal, where the spiral-shaped ramps have inspired their alternative name of 'snake bridges'.

The Industrial Revolution came and went, replaced by newer ideas and technologies that saw a decline in, among other things, horse-drawn transport. But although horses have become a rare sight on Britain's canals, they haven't disappeared completely. Children's author and narrowboat dweller Yarrow Townsend, who has spent her life outdoors among woodlands, waterways and stable yards, told me how easy it is for people to forget the whole canal system was built for horse-drawn boats. Many of the people who walk along urban canal routes don't know about this part of their history, especially as canal paths are now popular walking and cycling routes. But the clues are there if you look closely enough, as Yarrow has observed: 'Those of us who live and work on the canals, or have an interest in horses, will notice the little marks here and there – these remnants of horse-paced life. The grooves worn into iron railings on bridges – hollows thicker than your thumb, where the ropes have worn away at the metal year after year. The same marks can be found at the entrances to tunnels, too. I once moored my boat in Kintbury for a while, just outside Newbury, which is the only place I've seen a horse-drawn boat on the canal. It was used for tourist trips, and every few days I would hear the sound of giant hooves in the distance, driven by a man walking behind. Another man stood on the roof of the boat; his job was to lift the horse's rope over my boat and others', whose roofs were laden with obstacles like solar panels, TV aerials and, in my case, a pot full of mallows and sunflowers.

'Once,' Yarrow recalled, 'I was standing on a hill and looking down at them passing my boat. If I squinted, I could have imagined myself in the past – if it weren't for the sound of an A-road nearby, or the fact that the boat was loaded not with coal, but with passengers, each having a nosy at my boat garden or my pile of washing up. Having worked with rescue horses before, I found scenes like this sad; there just doesn't seem to be any room for horses on the canal anymore. There are far too many cyclists and ropes to trip over, not to mention dogs to be chased by or even, on occasion, the local hunt riding onto the towpath illegally, which can be frightening. Life on the canal is a slow one, but I would happily slow down even more for the privilege of travelling with a horse. It's a romantic idea, I know.'

Despite the slow, gentle nature of modern boating, it is also not as environmentally friendly as it could be. Most boaters, according to Yarrow, rely on diesel for propulsion, and the engines can be noisy as well as smelly: 'I wonder sometimes about clean air on the canals – what the future holds if we are ever able to leave fossil fuels behind. Sadly, even on the quietest stretches of the water, you would probably never be able to safely leave a horse grazing on the towpath beside the boat at night, as peaceful as that might sound. New forces shape the landscape now – the bikes and motorbikes, the mowers that come through and clear the wildflower banks to ensure things are "tidy". And like the rest of the countryside, towpaths are often very nitrogen rich due to dog walkers not clearing up after their pets, or because of agricultural run-off from nearby fields. This encourages an abundance of grass and nettles, and not so many rare plants; I suspect the landscape looks quite different now from what it once did.'

For those curious to experience horse-drawn boating, there are a small number of providers offering day trips around the nation's waterways. But the reality is that horses are rarely seen on the towpaths anymore – a consequence of modernity, of course, but perhaps also a reflection of our twenty-first century need for speed and efficiency. Just as encouraging more horses on to our roads would be an impractical way to cling to the past, so too are our canals currently an unfit place for most horses to live and work. But the future is an unwritten page, and as we attempt to cut ourselves adrift from our reliance on fossil fuels, who knows in which direction we will go? If the last few years have taught us anything, it is that society is more capable of change than we might think.

CHAPTER SIX

Equestrienne

There is a pretty village near my town in the sweeping South Downs called Hawkley, speckled with houses and a church, a good pub and a village green. It's very *Midsomer Murders*, without the murders; the kind of affluent countryside to which you'd like to escape at the weekend and enjoy a long dog walk, followed swiftly by a crisp glass of wine. At the back of the village, beyond the cricket pavilion, there is a wide expanse of open field known locally as the Gallops, which, unsurprisingly, is one of the best local places to do exactly as the name suggests. In the south-east particularly, there are fewer spaces with open access for riders that aren't heavily used by dog walkers and cyclists, too – places where you can worry less about who you're sharing the path with, and really enjoy the feeling of a horse travelling beneath you. Hawkley's Gallops is one of these places – the space is so open and the visibility so good, that if another walker or cyclist rightfully joined the path, you would have plenty of time to slow down and continue safely. The Gallops are where I, and many others, have come as close as humanly possible to experiencing the unconstrained speed of a horse at full pelt.

When I first rode alone with Roxy to the Gallops, I had no plans for a speedy ride. I liked to think I was a fairly capable horsewoman, able to handle Roxy calmly and enjoy a controlled canter at a relaxed pace. I had ridden through many fields similar to this one, full of tempting stretches of open land that any horse would love to lollop through, but I had no reason to think this would be a particularly wild one. What, then, made it so different? My only conclusion was that there must be something in the air here that only horses could detect. A collective energy about the place, full of

memory and vitality; an urge that crept into the head of
every horse that came here and told them to just GO. As
soon as we stepped onto the track that ran around the edge
of the field, I felt the reins tighten and knew Roxy wanted
to move. Keep it cool, I told myself. You are a horsewoman!
You are in charge! But was I really? Perhaps a better way to
put it was that I had hopefully gained enough of Roxy's
respect that she was willing to follow my lead – but the
truth was that, like any horse, she was a huge, powerful
animal that could do anything she wanted at any time. I
could sense that every inch of her wanted to run, and I had
a choice – I could clasp those reins the whole way around
the field, attempt a jolty sort of canter, exhaust us both in
doing so, and somehow call it a good ride if I didn't fall off.
Or I could trust her intuition to let us both have a bit of fun.
There was nobody else on the path, no obstacles in the way
and no good reason not to, so I released the tension in the
reins, relaxed into the saddle and away we went.

The difficulty of riding a galloping horse is that, despite
travelling up to 30mph on a live animal that can trip over,
change direction or buck you off at any moment, you are
absolutely obliged to relax. The more anxious you are, the
more tense your body is, and the less able you are to move
your legs, hips and core with the rhythm of the horse's gait.
I felt the thud of Roxy's hooves transition from a three-beat
canter to the four-beat gallop, and no longer able to stay in
the saddle without being bumped out, I stood up in the
stirrups so I was crouching over her shoulders. And it was at
this point that the ride became more comfortable, because
although I was hurtling forward at a more startling speed, all
I had to focus on was keeping my legs strong and my body
steady. Finding the rhythm, holding on, letting go. And
when I finally managed to look up and take in the view
through Roxy's ears, it felt like total freedom. Swathes of
grass and blossoming hedgerows rushing past, a white sky
above and the warm, beating body of a horse beneath my

legs. It was exhilarating and peaceful and powerful, all at once. We galloped along the edge of the field and up to the top corner, where we stopped at last and looked down across the South Downs and beyond, both catching our breaths in the morning sun.

℧

It is difficult not to feel empowered when sitting astride a horse. They elevate you in more ways than just your physical height; they enrich your mental and physical presence, and they make you feel powerful. It is why the police force still uses mounted officers in crowds, events and urban patrols. Many of us find a police officer intimidating (anyone else see the police and become immediately convinced they've committed a crime?), but a police officer on a horse is a potent image, and their presence alone has been proven to deter criminals. As a woman who enjoys spending time outdoors, I find riding gives me the confidence to cope with the negative aspects of being alone in the countryside. Most, if not all, women know the dangers of being outside alone, in both rural and urban landscapes. It isn't even something we consciously learn; the society in which we live has burned into us that women are more likely to feel unsafe outside their home, no matter the location, time of day, choice of clothes, age or general behaviour. A 2021 study by the Office for National Statistics showed that two out of three women aged 16 to 34 experienced one form of harassment in the previous 12 months; 44 per cent of women from the same survey had experienced catcalls, whistles, unwanted sexual comments or jokes, and 29 per cent had felt, at least once, that they were being followed. Women today are more encouraged to stay home after dark, to not use taxis alone, to keep their phones charged at all times, to not drink too much; all sensible suggestions in their own way, but all things that men rarely have to think

about. It may feel less dangerous to be out in the countryside
in broad daylight, sober and alert with a charged phone and
body protector, but even then, we are conditioned as
women to never totally let our guard down; we can never
be fully allowed to breathe, to relax, to be alone in the
world without having to wonder if we are, in fact, alone.
And there lies the reason why riding is so liberating –
because when we go out hacking into the deep, dark woods
alone, we're not really alone at all. Our horses are our
companions; we may not speak the same verbal language,
but they are with us for every quiet lane, every blind corner,
every step that leads us out and away from home, and all the
way back again.

During the seventeenth and eighteenth centuries, it was
uncommon, although not unheard of, for a woman of a
higher social class to be wandering outside alone without a
servant or companion. The influence of social etiquette
stifled women who had any care for their social standing,
their reputation and choice of potential suitors, as in doing
so they were at risk of being labelled suspicious, dishonest
and unchaste. Although women did travel alone, at home
and abroad, they were usually older, widowed or unmarried,
and free of the great expectations of their youth. Horse
riding, on the other hand, was one of the only socially
acceptable physical activities for girls and women of the
upper classes, right up until the 1850s. Similarly to walking,
it wasn't common for women to ride out alone – especially
without a servant – but regardless of the company they kept,
imagine the freedom riding must have given these women
of the upper-middle classes. Women whose every move,
word, outfit and opinion was analysed by their social circle,
and who lived in a world where it was forbidden to publicly
express any kind of sexual urge. Imagine the feeling of
mounting a horse – an animal driven only by instinct and
intuition – and flying across the country on thundering

hooves, heart beating, skirts shivering, and the chance to feel the elements roaring in full force against your face and body.

For many women, their day-to-day riding pursuits would have had to be enough to satisfy any lust for adventure – but for others, it was only the beginning. One of the most-renowned female equestriennes, Celia Fiennes, embarked on a series of horseback journeys, between 1685 and 1703, that would take her through every county in England. Recording the sights and experiences in her journal, and with a particular fascination for industrial communities and processes, her writing was posthumously published as the celebrated memoir *Through England on a Side Saddle in the Time of William and Mary*, which has since been dubbed by Professor Andrew McRae in his book *Literature and Domestic Travel in Early Modern England* as the 'most important travel journal of the seventeenth century'. Fiennes' interests lay in both the domestic affairs of everyday life and in the industries that were driving the country forward into a bold but unfamiliar future. In her desire to learn as much as she could about her native land, but also to engage with the latest innovations, she visited newly fashionable spa towns, witnessed the construction of fine baroque country houses, visited cheesemakers, potteries, paper mills and tin mines, counted the stones at Stonehenge, and even climbed the rocks at Land's End. Fiennes' patriotic interest in exploring her homeland as a tourist, as well as her interest in the industries found along the way, anticipated the literary genre of 'economic tourism', a staple of the travel writing canon in the eighteenth and nineteenth centuries. Writers like Samuel Pepys, John Evelyn, Daniel Defoe, who wrote his *Tour Through the Whole Island of Great Britain* later in 1726, and William Cobbett, whose *Rural Rides* inspired the idea for the book you are reading now, overshadowed Fiennes' contribution to travel writing for many years; it is only recently that her work has been credited as one of the most extensive and detailed accounts of English society in the seventeenth century.

Although more women would set out on similar journeys over the coming decades, Fiennes' travels were nothing short of remarkable considering the time in which she lived. They marked the start of a trend in British women taking the opportunity to explore, not only their own landscapes at home, but those further afield. Their desire to explore the great outdoors was able to extend beyond the confines of the British Isles and take many female adventurers to places all over the world. And with horses as one of their main modes of transport, they were able to enjoy this freedom within the relative security of a conventionally acceptable pastime like equestrianism. These 'pilgrimages' were not, however, universally accepted by all. In the wake of the Protestant Reformation, which swept through Europe in the 1500s, the Catholic culture of pilgrimage was condemned. In 1520, leading reformer Martin Luther declared:

All pilgrimages should be stopped. There is no good in them: no commandment enjoins them, no obedience attaches to them. Rather do these pilgrimages give countless occasions to commit sin and to despise God's commandments.

The idea of pilgrimage, however – especially for those who weren't devoutly religious – still drew people in, although it later became less about visiting holy places and more about travelling to see the marvels, or *curiositas*, of the world. When Celia Fiennes decided to ride through every county in England, however, the image of the pilgrim or wandering traveller, moving without any quantifiable purpose, was still viewed with suspicion. This meant that the roads had become less hospitable for lone travellers, on top of the routes being poorly marked, narrow, often flooded, overgrown and plagued by robbers. Combined with the fact that she was an unmarried woman travelling without a male companion of her own social station, and accompanied by only two servants, the decision to make a journey of this kind would not have been taken lightly.

Between her notes on the people and places she encountered, we find details of her daily riding experiences – out on her horse all day, every day – and the troubles and freedoms they brought her. We hear of an encounter with what were likely opportunistic highwaymen, jostling between her and her servant's horses to try and cause confusion. She laments the need for her horse to be reshod every two to three days due to poor roads, and celebrates one smithy whose final shoe lasted six weeks. She accepts her horse's refusal to go near the sulphur well at Harrogate, which she agrees smells 'like carrion'; and she rides over the Vale of White Horse to see the Uffington chalk figure, 'which is Cutt out the shape off a horse in perfect proportions in broad wayes, and is seen a great distance very plaine'. One of her most remarkable observations takes place in Coventry, when she sees:

> The statue of a man Looking out of a window wth his Eyes out, and is a monument as history tell us of some priviledges obtein'd by a Lady wife, to the nobleman who was lord of ye town, and she was to purchase them by passing on horse back through ye town naked wch he thought she would not do, but out of zeale to relieve ye town from some hard bondage she did, and Commanded all windows and doores to be shutt and none to appear in the streete on pain of death wch was obey'd by all; but one man would open a window and Looke out and for his impudence had this judgment on him to be struck blind; this statue is his resemblance and one day in a year they Remember ye good Lady by some rejoyceing.

The 'Lady wife' to whom she is referring is none other than Lady Godiva, a gentlewoman of Anglo-Saxon origin best remembered for riding her horse naked through the streets of

Coventry. According to legend, Lady Godiva had implored her husband Leofric to reduce Coventry's heavy taxes. He declared he would do so only if she rode naked on horseback through the town, a demand to which she agreed. Covering her body with her long, beautiful hair, she ordered the townspeople to stay inside and lock the doors, warning that anyone caught watching her would be sentenced to death. All obeyed the order except one – a man caught peering out of the window, who was later struck blind as punishment. The man became known as Peeping Tom, and Lady Godiva's husband, so astonished by his wife's actions, was said to have freed the town from all tolls – except those for horses. Now engraved in local legend, the story has been re-enacted in some form every year since the seventeenth century, and in 1949, a bronze statue of Lady Godiva and her horse was unveiled in the heart of the city. It was named *Self Sacrifice*.

U

Celia Fiennes, and others like her, set the stage for more women to explore the landscape on their own terms. One of these was Marianne North, an English artist and adventurer who travelled twice around the world by herself, often on horseback, at a time when women weren't allowed to vote and very few were well educated. Financially comfortable but unmarried ('Marriage?' she once wrote. 'A terrible experiment.'), North found company tiresome and conventional life in England even more so, particularly within the limitations of her social circles. She once wrote to her sister how she often found female company difficult, referencing the 'unthinking croqueting-badminton young ladies' whose conversation was perhaps too shallow and unacademic. A lifelong lover of art and nature, at the age of 40, shortly after the death of her father, who had always supported her work, she set off on a series of journeys on horseback that would occupy the rest of her life.

North's travels took her across the world, from Chile and Brazil to India and Japan, from Madagascar and Seychelles to Australia and New Zealand. She had a passion for painting tropical flowers and plants in their natural environments, an unusual choice at the time when most botanical paintings were set against white backgrounds to draw more attention to the main subject. Wherever she was in the world, North would wake at dawn and take tea outside to watch the day begin. She would then paint outdoors frantically until noon, once describing the process as 'a vice like dram-drinking, almost impossible to leave off once it gets possession of one'. On rainy days she painted indoors, but in good weather she would spend her afternoons and evenings exploring until well after dark. Hers was a life, she declared, of 'wander and wonder and paint!' North especially loved travelling on foot or by horseback, with or without a side-saddle, as she preferred a slower means of travel that also allowed her to see the world from a different perspective. Her only rule, she wrote, was never to go 'willingly anywhere where I could not see my feet'.

By the end of her life, North had completed 832 paintings of over 1,000 specimens from around the world. As the number grew, she regularly sent them to be exhibited at the Kew Gallery in the Royal Botanic Gardens in London; eventually, she paid for a gallery to be built at Kew, known as the Marianne North Gallery, where her paintings are still on display today. It is the only permanent space dedicated to a single female artist's work in Britain and, when writing to North in 1884, Queen Victoria called it 'a gift to the nation' – although there were still many at the time who struggled with the idea that the gallery was the work of one woman. North once wrote about the work it took to get the exhibition up and running, but that she didn't mind because it had brought her into contact with so many interesting people, including one gentleman who wandered into the gallery by mistake and turned to her to ask: 'It isn't true what they say about these being painted by one woman, is it?' North confirmed that it was she who had painted them all, upon which he seized both her hands and said: 'You! Then it is lucky for you that you did not live two hundred years ago, or you would have been burnt for a witch.'

At a time when colour photography was still uncommon, we can only imagine how mesmerising North's paintings must have been to the general public, many of whom had never ventured beyond England, let alone beyond Europe. The fact that they were also painted in oil, rather than the more traditional and 'feminine' watercolours, fascinated her contemporaries. Watercolours would have been preferable for capturing the tiniest details of the plants, but oil allowed her to work in daring, vibrant colours, much more accurate to the plants she would have been observing. Living at the height of the British Empire, the circles North moved in would have also been full of men in search of new and exotic specimens to bring back to English soil, either to grow in their glasshouses or preserve, dead, in their collections. In contrast, North was far more interested in visual capture through art, rather than physically taking the plants away. Her focus was on the connection between trees, plants and flowers and their environments, and for her the beauty lay in this interconnectivity more than the specimens themselves. When Sir Joseph Hooker, a friend of Darwin and the director at Kew for 20 years, wrote about the importance of North's paintings, he focused not on the art itself, but on its power to inspire viewers:

> On the beauty of the collection it is unnecessary to dwell ... Visitors may, however, be glad to be reminded that very many of the views here brought together represent vividly and truthful scenes of astonishing interest and singularity, and objects that are among the wonders of the vegetable

kingdom; and that these, though now accessible to travellers
and familiar to readers of travel, are already disappearing, or
are doomed shortly to disappear, before the axe and the
forest fires, the plough and the flock, of the ever advancing
settler or colonist. Such scenes can never be renewed by
nature, nor when once effaced can they be pictured to the
mind's eye, except by means of such records as this lady has
presented to us, and to posterity.

The idea of conserving nature may not have been as much
of a hot topic as it is today, but North's work was valued by
people like Hooker for drawing people into the natural
world and inspiring them to take better care of it. Certainly,
plants captured her heart in a way that nothing else could,
and in all her written material it is always the plants that
evoke the richest, most passionate responses to day-to-day
life. One such event takes place while North is riding her
horse through the gold mining hills of Cata Branca in
Brazil, when she spots some rare plants between the rocks
and identifies one, from horseback, as *Macrosiphonia longiflora*,
a plant with delicate white flowers that she later describes
with nothing short of infatuation: 'like a giant white
primrose of rice-paper with a throat three inches long; it
was mounted on a slender stalk, and had leaves of white
plush like our mullein, and a most delicious scent of cloves
… I was getting wild with my longing to dismount and
examine these'. North later describes a set of pitcher plants
in Singapore that make her 'scream with delight'. In a
society that kept every whisper of sexuality behind closed
doors, it is easy to find the sensuality of the natural world
revealed in North's paintings. But regardless of whether she
intentionally wove those ideas into her work, we can only
imagine the freedom North must have felt as a lone woman
of her time, exploring the world one tropical plant at a
time, with little more than a horse, a suitcase and a
paintbrush to drive her forward.

Although her exotic pursuit of adventure was unusual for the time, North's interest in botany was not. The study of plant life was a popular and commendable pastime for Victorian girls and women, and while they rarely received formal training on the subject – that privilege being reserved for boys – they were still encouraged to learn about plants by collecting, pressing, studying, drawing, painting and systemising them. Not only was botany inexpensive and genteel, it was considered pious for young ladies to study the work of their creator, especially as they could learn about the natural world without seeing animals copulating or killing each other. It was also a healthy form of outdoor exercise, and one in which people could respectably meet with members of the opposite sex. During the Victorian era, people of all ages could be seen gallivanting about the countryside, collecting and documenting specimens with a passion best remembered by a phenomenon known as Pteridomania, or 'fern fever'. This obsession with capturing ferns spread across Britain, Europe and the Americas, leading to accidents, fatalities and the near disappearance of several rare species.

Over the pond in the United States, another pair of equestrians were also hit by the Victorian fern fever and the general thirst for botany at the time. The couple, husband John Gill Lemmon and his wife Sara Plummer, fell in love over their shared passion for plants, and for their honeymoon decided to ride horseback through the Catalina mountains near Tucson, Arizona. So rare was it for a woman to be involved in such an expedition, local historians even recorded the clothing Sara wore:

> A short suit of strong material, the best of firm calfskin shoes, nailed along the soles and heels with jump tacks and reinforced by substantial leather leggings that promised defiance to cacti and snakes. A broad brimmed hat with a buckskin mask and heavy gloves, a botanical folio, and a long staff completed her outfit.

The couple had already survived a plant-hunting trip in which they were forced to hide in makeshift tunnels while Apache war tribes searched the Californian hills for white invaders, so their choice of honeymoon had to be something special. After one failed attempt on foot, the locals supplied them with horses and they tried again. By the time the trip was over they had fought off rattlesnakes, escaped chasms and rockslides, navigated fields of cacti in extreme temperatures, crossed deserts, slept in horse-thief territory and completely run out of supplies. They did, however, reach the summit of a valley they believed was a botanist's paradise, where their guide 'chopped the bark off a great pine tree on the very top' on which they all carved their names. Arizona's Mount Lemmon was eventually named after Sara, who rode up it on horseback to the summit. It remains one of the only mountains named after a woman, which is some consolation as many of the couple's initial discoveries of the area were credited only to 'John Gill Lemmon & Wife'. On returning home to Oakland, the couple continued their botanical work together; Sara would later go on to influence the adoption of the golden poppy as the state flower of California.

One of the best-known equestrienne travellers of the Victorian era was Isabella Bird, an eccentric explorer with phenomenal energy, failing health and a preference for the most dangerous adventures she could find: comparing them to the feeling of falling in love. Like North, she travelled alone and very lightly, bringing just a few clothes and personal items, a good supply of tea, dried soup and a sweetener known as saccharin. She was also the first woman to ever address the Royal Geographical Society in 1892; its members deemed her 'the most accomplished traveller of her time'. Having suffered from poor health and spinal problems from an early age, she spent many years in bed after having a tumour removed before the doctors suggested she try travelling to help relieve her pain. Her first trip was to the United States, and from the moment she left England, her health improved and the world opened up to her, prompting her to write her first book in 1856, *The English Woman in America*.

Bird's spinal injury flared up again when she returned to England, and after her parents' deaths she decided first to travel to Australia, and then what was formerly the Sandwich Islands (now known as Hawaii), where she noticed how the women there rode their horses astride instead of side-saddle. Intrigued, she tried it herself – and, perhaps unsurprisingly, her back pain quickly disappeared. From then on, she rode astride everywhere she went, next travelling on horseback over the Rocky Mountains and learning to drive wagons and herd cattle. She hiked up peaks, became trapped by snow in a cabin through the winter, and wrote her fourth and most popular book, *A Lady's Life in the Rocky Mountains*. Aside from an eight-year spell of marriage, her travels continued through Asia, including to Japan, China, Korea, Vietnam, Malaya, India, Tibet, Persia, Kurdistan and Turkey. She also travelled among the Berbers in Morocco, where the sultan gifted her a black stallion so tall that she required a ladder to mount it. In Asia, she even tried riding elephants through the rivers and forests; at one point, she became submerged up to her neck in water, later writing of the incident: 'this mode of riding is not comfortable'.

A pioneer of adventure and stepping out of her comfort zone, Bird's love of horses was enriched by her courage to defy social convention and ride astride instead of side-saddle – a choice that not only saved her health, but gave her the freedom she so desperately wanted to explore the world. By the early twentieth century, riding astride (or 'cross-saddle') was becoming more common, although it was not until after the First World War that it became the social norm. When the war broke out, an article in *The Times* highlighted this clash between traditional and progressive femininity all over Europe:

The Kaiser's order expressing his desire that the wives of German Army officers shall immediately discontinue the practice of riding astride is being very widely and keenly discussed by horsewomen all over the country. The fact that it comes soon after King George's refusal to witness any exhibition of riding astride at Olympia is regarded as significant.

The truth is that women were riding astride for centuries before the side-saddle was introduced. The phenomenon is commonly attributed to Queen Anne of Bohemia, who rode across Europe in 1382 to marry King Richard II, sitting on a small padded seat with a footrest called a planchette. While some suggest Queen Anne only rode in this way because of a disability, or because she did not want to risk her virginity being called into question before her wedding, her royal status popularised riding sideways, encouraging others to follow the trend until it was not only more fashionable to ride side-saddle – it was dishonourable not to. Side-saddle became associated with femininity and modesty, as well as helping to keep the rider's hymen intact and therefore promoting their virgin status. In hindsight, it led to centuries of women riding precariously and uncomfortably, all to uphold a toxic and unrealistic image of womanhood. An 1801 issue of *The Sporting Magazine* worded the situation perfectly:

> [Queen Anne of Bohemia] managed to abolish the safe, commodious, and natural mode of riding hitherto practised by the women of England, and to introduce the sidesaddle.

Between the fourteenth and twentieth centuries, side-saddle was considered the only socially acceptable way for ladies to ride across western Europe and beyond. In 1903, Alice M. Hayes wrote *The Horsewoman: A Practical Guide to Side-Saddle Riding*, and touched on the question of riding astride – an idea she did not consider to be worth entertaining:

I have studied the art of riding astride in an ordinary man's saddle, and would give a negative answer to that query. The fact that by the adoption of the cross saddle, about seven pounds in weight would be saved, and the work for the horse would be somewhat easier, ought not to outweigh the enormous disadvantages on the other side. Whenever a lady is dragged by skirt or stirrup and killed – an accident which, happily, occurs but rarely nowadays, for we wisely adopt the best safety appliances to prevent – up crops that evergreen question of cross-saddle riding, as if men never come to grief! ... A woman's limbs are unsuited to cross-saddle riding, which requires length from hip to knee, flat muscles, and a slight inclination to 'bow legs'. I practised my cross-saddle riding in a school well supplied with large mirrors in which I could see my figure as I passed. It was anything but graceful, for the rotundity, which even in some men is very ugly on horseback, was far too much *en évidence*, and caused an outburst of laughter from the ladies who were watching my performance.

Fortunately, the stigma around riding astride did not stop some women doing it anyway, although if they were socialites or celebrities in the public eye, they were almost always tarnished as being too masculine, attention-seeking or frivolous. Perhaps one of the most famous examples was Marie Antoinette, the last Queen of France to rule before the French Revolution. After learning to ride in order to hunt with her husband, she abandoned the long flowing skirts of a side-saddle rider, and wore slim breeches instead; women did wear breeches for riding, but they were typically hidden underneath more 'feminine' skirts and petticoats. Her mother, the Empress Maria Theresa, pleaded with her to dress more appropriately – and even to stop riding altogether:

Riding spoils the complexion, and in the end your waistline will suffer from it and begin to show more noticeably.

Furthermore, if you are riding like a man, dressed as a man, as I suspect you are, I have to tell you that I find it dangerous as well as bad for bearing children – and that is what you have been called upon to do; that will be the measure of your success.

Fortunately for Queen Marie, her exploits did not in fact prevent her from bearing children, although sadly only one out of four made it to adulthood. In 1783, the artist Louis–Auguste Brun painted her on horseback, dressed in the blue hunting habit of the Palace of Versailles; audaciously, Brun painted her riding astride and wearing slim breeches, her horse rearing boldly and powerfully. Her defiance of traditional riding etiquette would later come back to haunt her as 'proof' of her insatiable thirst for power and even her alleged lesbianism, but for a time, at least, her boldness won the hearts of the French people, who would travel for miles to catch a glimpse of their Queen riding through the city.

Back in England, it was not so easy to embrace riding astride without being subjected to ridicule. The diarist Samuel Pepys once described how, upon visiting Whitehall Palace, he noticed with displeasure how the women there were dressed:

In their riding garbs, with coats and doublets and deep skirts, just for all the world like men, and buttoned their doublets up to the breast, with periwigs[6] and with hats; so that, only for a long petticoat dragging under their men's coats, nobody could take them for women in any point whatever – which was an odd sight, and a sight which did not please me.

---

[6] The periwig was a highly styled wig worn by both women and men in the mid to late eighteenth century. They were often made of horsehair.

Poor Mr Pepys would have been horrified, then, at one more equestrienne adventurer, who not only rode astride and wore breeches but also campaigned for women's suffrage, women's football, amendments to marriage and divorce laws, Irish home rule, who openly shared her political opinions, and – worst of all – spoke passionately about the need for true equality between men and women.

Born in 1855, Lady Florence Dixie was a Scottish writer, war correspondent, suffragist and traveller. In December 1878, just two months after the birth of her second son, Dixie and her husband (Sir Alexander Beaumont Churchill Dixie – he is never mentioned by name, only as 'my husband'), together with her two brothers and a family friend, set off on a journey that would take them thousands of miles across the globe, and away from home for months. Their destination was Patagonia, the southernmost tip of South America where arid grassland and desert meet dramatic mountain peaks, glacial fjords and rainforests. Even today, it is wild, barren and beautiful, but when Dixie and her party arrived there almost 200 years ago, it was one of the only places in the world that was still considered 'untouched' by Europeans, and one that Dixie delighted in, allowing her to leave the 'shallow artificiality of modern existence':

> Nowhere else are you so completely alone. Nowhere else is there an area of 100,000 square miles which you may gallop over, and where, whilst enjoying a healthy, bracing climate, you are safe from the persecutions of fevers, friends, savage tribes, obnoxious animals, telegrams, letters, and every other nuisance... To these attractions was added the thought, always alluring to an active mind, that there too I should be able to penetrate into vast wilds, virgin as yet to the foot of man.[7]

---

[7] Patagonia was not, of course, virgin to the foot of man; Dixie's comment belongs to the larger imperialist attitude of the time that the only man worth mentioning in this context was European.

The journey was completed almost entirely on horseback, which meant 12–13 hours in the saddle every day, travelling, hunting game and escaping the dangers they met along the way. But despite being the only woman in the group, Dixie proved herself to be just as active and resilient as the others – and just as hungry for adventure. Galloping across the steppes by day and sleeping under the stars each night, Dixie documented the journey in her best-selling book *Across Patagonia* (1881). She hunted guanaco and ostrich, battled extreme temperatures, gnats and mosquitoes, fought off pumas, tracked feral horses, and once became engulfed in a huge wildfire that swept through the plains. Never complaining and always game for the next adventure, by the end of her journey she had even found herself two new pets to bring back to England: a stray dog called Pucho, and a jaguar she called Affums (which ended up killing several deer in Windsor Great Park and had to be sent to a zoo).

Dixie's love for far-flung horseback travel was unusual for a woman of the late nineteenth century, as she herself observes in the first chapter of her book when she recalls other people's reactions when she told them the news: "'Patagonia! who would ever think of going to such a place?'" "'Why, you will be eaten up by cannibals!'" But within the context of her life as a whole, an adventure like this one seems almost commonplace. A highly intelligent, capable and confident woman, she rebelled against the oppressive expectations of women, and sought out knowledge in a way women weren't encouraged to. On returning from Patagonia, Dixie even wrote to Charles Darwin to offer her observations on the tuco-tuco, a burrowing rodent she encountered on her journey. Darwin had described the animal as rarely venturing above ground, but Dixie assured him she had seen five or six of them at a time outside their burrows on moonlit nights. In 1881, she became a war correspondent for a British newspaper and was sent to South Africa to cover the Anglo–Zulu War, and in 1895 she became the first president of the British Ladies' Football Club. She was a fierce advocate for equality, campaigning for women's suffrage and writing a best-selling novel, *Gloriana*, about a feminist utopian future.

During her early life, Dixie was also known for her love of blood sports. She was an intrepid rider and a good shot, and admitted that part of the reason she was drawn to fox hunting was because it put her on a level playing field with her male peers. So skilfully did she ride, in fact, that she was mentioned in sporting magazines more than once. In later life, however, her views changed completely, and in 1905 she published *The Horrors of Sport*, a book that condemned blood sports as cruel and barbaric. She went on to become a supporter of the Humanitarian League and vice president of the London Vegetarian Association, spending the rest of her life campaigning for fairness and equality for both women and animals. In her 1904 essay *Towards Freedom*, published a year before her death, she wrote:

> Those who desire to see a reign of love take the place of one just the reverse, desire humanity to face the truth and build upon it a sane religion and sane laws, whose composition shall contain true love, in which real justice, kindness, mercy, and fair play to all are alone embowered.

Few women of her time enjoyed the same privileges as Lady Florence Dixie; not only was she financially comfortable enough to travel for months at a time, she was also so highly esteemed in her social circles that she could seek freedom and fairness without damaging her reputation. Her life was a relatively short one – she died of diphtheria at the age of 50 – but she spent every moment of it in search of adventure and freedom, galloping across the world and seeing it all through a wider, more compassionate lens than many of her contemporaries. Above everything else, she understood the value of true wilderness and the beauty that lies within the untouched, unpolluted places of the Earth, as we learn from the final chapter of *Across Patagonia*, when she reflects on her journey:

> I remember the days when, after a long and weary ride, I slept, pillowed on my saddle, the open sky above me, a sounder and sweeter sleep than I had ever slept before.

Grateful for the experiences she had, Dixie's writing captures the joy of finding freedom in the comfort of a saddle; the chance, in a society that so carefully controlled a woman's access to knowledge, to witness first-hand the magic and wonder of the natural world.

CHAPTER SEVEN

The Fair

A row of 16 ponies stood tied to the metal fence outside the old pub, each with a straw braid woven into their tails, strung with red, white and blue ribbons. I asked a young man standing nearby what the braids were for. He couldn't have been older than 17, dressed in tweed with a horse whip under his arm, friendly and polite but, for whatever reason, unable to look me directly in the eye. I was one of very few women here, and one of only a few not accompanied by a man; I wondered if this made him uncomfortable, but he was happy to chat, nonetheless. He told me the braids were traditional for Fair Day, and that many of the owners would have been up since dawn getting their horses ready. The morning's drizzle had given them a slightly dishevelled look, but generally they all looked pretty relaxed considering they were standing on an A-road in the middle of a busy Hampshire village. It wasn't as busy as you would usually find it on a Friday in May, of course. The village of Wickham was a popular place seven days a week, but today, every pub, café and shop was closed, except for a mobile burger and coffee van that had popped up between the horses and the fairground rides. And aside from the fairgoers themselves, you could tell there were very few locals here, the majority staying behind closed doors until the events of the day had passed. A stark contrast to the usual farmers' markets or country fairs that grace English towns like these, always bustling with shoppers, browsers and swarms of cheese-samplers. More surprising was the fact that this was the oldest horse fair in the country. In 1269, a royal charter was granted by King Henry III to hold a weekly market here, and the horse fair alongside it was born. So what made this rural tradition so different to all the others?

Unlike mainstream shows and markets, the Wickham Horse Fair was organised and attended by members of the Gypsy, Roma and Traveller (GRT) community.[8] Traditionally, the horses are lined up along the road for potential buyers to inspect, then when their turn comes, they are paraded down the running track (usually the A334), either with their grooms jogging alongside, riding the horses bareback, or hitched onto a sulky (a light, two-wheeled horse-drawn cart designed for one or two people, often used for trotting races). Similar to what occurs at the larger and better known Appleby Horse Fair held in Cumbria in mid-June, horse traders come to the fair from all corners of the country, with most as interested in enjoying a community gathering as they are in buying or selling horses. But the connection between horse and Traveller is still deeply rooted: 'Gypsy gold does not chink and glitter. It gleams in the sun and neighs in the dark,' so goes the saying commonly attributed to the Claddagh Gypsies of Galway, Ireland. Despite Travellers being one of the most enigmatic communities in the British Isles and beyond, romanticised and demonised in equal measure, there are some aspects of the culture that have become so iconic, any outsider would be able to recognise them. One of these is the pairing of the Traveller and his horse; another, perhaps, is the brightly painted vardo caravan that once heralded their arrival, dating from the mid-1800s through to the early twentieth century, a time celebrated by Romanichal Travellers (a Romani subgroup within the UK) as the 'wagon years'.

I spoke to the writer and Traveller Damian Le Bas about the relationship between Travellers and their horses; his 2018

---

[8] 'Traveller' is an umbrella term for several different ethnic communities, including Gypsies, Roma and Irish Travellers. The word 'gypsy' is controversial and has historically been used as a racial slur, so it has not been used except when quoting somebody else or using an established nominal term like 'Gypsy cob'. For simplicity, I will be hereafter using the word 'Traveller' to refer to the Gypsy, Roma and Traveller community.

book *The Stopping Places: A Journey through Gypsy Britain* follows in the horse-drawn tracks of his own ancestors as they pursued a tough and largely nomadic existence on the open road: 'For so long,' he explained, 'the horse was so many things to the Gypsies. During the wagon years in particular (and for a few people the wagon years have never really ended), the horse had a combination of roles that seems very strange, as if one animal should not be able to play all these parts at once. The horse was transport, of course, but not just transport in the way it is to the rider. By pulling the wagon, drawing it from a place which had become less appropriate to a new place that was now a better option, it was the means by which the home was kept secure. Through its strength and its movement and stoical labour the horse played a guardian's role. Everyone that lived in the wagon, or slept underneath it, depended on the horse to make sure it remained a good home: the horse literally drew it to safety, away from threats.'

And it was not only their physical strength that bonded Traveller families to their horses over the centuries. Damian explained how horses have long been valued companions for children in the Traveller community. 'They are honoured pets,' he explains, 'and even part of the family.' As many Travellers bought and sold horses for a living, for many families, the horse literally put food on the table. To some, this dual approach to the horse might seem strange, as if it speaks of an attitude wherein true respect for the animal is lacking. But for Damian, it's a unique relationship: 'I'd prefer to see it as mercurial and even magical, the way a non-human being could be so vital to a people in so many ways.'

Damian is reminded of something the filmmaker Phillip Donnellan said in the 1960s: 'The Gypsy can't get away from the horse.' He tells me how his relatives have long kept horses, even though they are no longer practical and says he hopes to have his own again one day. 'Even if I don't do much with them besides standing at the edge of a field and stroking their coats, it's an instant cure to a lot of malaises.'

Damian calls this 'socialising' with horses and shared that he wasn't surprised to learn that spending time with horses is now a form of therapy for mental health issues. Equine therapy, as it has become known, is proven to instil a strong sense of companionship, comfort and wellbeing in patients, many of whom go on to successfully process and change negative behaviours. Damian acknowledged that some Travellers had knowingly treated the horse as nothing but a beast of burden or a commodity to buy or sell, but that for many in his community, the bond was much deeper: 'There is a lot of history behind the chrome horseshoe that Travellers fasten to the grille of their Transit truck.'

For Raine Geoghegan, a poet, prose writer and playwright of Romani, Welsh and Irish descent, horses also played an important role in her ancestral stories. She told me how both her maternal and paternal grandparents, the Lanes and the Ripleys, were horse dealers in Kent and the East End, buying and selling *grai* (horses) but always keeping their favourite ones. At Traveller funerals, where it is popular to opt for a horse-drawn hearse, they plait the mane and tail then put a feather in the head-strap. The hearse for Raine's second cousin's grandmother was pulled by two beautiful black horses, and drew such a crowd that it was even filmed by a local TV station. As a writer, she feels that her Romani heritage has brought her closer to nature and the landscapes of home, from the fields in which her family picked hops every autumn, to the early mornings boiling water for tea around the *yog* (fire) and the nights preparing food and listening to the owls in the darkness. 'I have written about my family extensively as a way to reconnect with my ancestors, and nature has become central to this,' she explained. 'I look upon nature as a mirror and I see a reflection of who I am or who I want to be. Nature is a spiritual pathway, a guide, a healing presence. I know this was true for my ancestors. They may have lived in vardos but the wild fields and pathways were their true home.'

Raine's creative work has also confirmed her belief that horses have always been very special to her people, intertwined with the open road, the wilderness and the desire for freedom. 'They represent the complex relationship between movement, freedom and ownership,' she observed. 'They have a power which transcends any other way of travelling. It's the old way. The horse leads the way, the people and wagons follow. And the horses that are well groomed and clearly loved by their family look beautiful as they lead the wagons along the road. My granny was very proud of the first horse that she and my grandfather bought to go with their wagon after they were married. It was a big investment and they looked after it well. My grandfather said that he spoke to his horses and they responded in different ways, because they were usually seen as part of the family. I think they also symbolised a certain kind of power, perhaps on a level closer to the soul. For example, they would often be ridden bareback, and because there were so many restrictions on Gypsy people, I wonder if riding a horse in this way was a form of rebellion. I am reminded of the New Forest Gypsies who were surrounded by free-roaming horses, and I feel that must have been significant to them, echoing the freedom they longed for, too.' Although not a regular rider herself, the interconnection between horses and Traveller culture means that horses have found their way into Raine's work many times, including her beautiful piece 'Kushti Grai', written in memory of Michael Edward O'Neil, a Traveller who lived in Carlisle and bought a former warhorse called Mad Alf, which had shell shock from its time serving in the First World War:

'Kushti Grai'

He was called Mad Alf, on account of 'im bein' on the nervous side. He couldn't stand still,
'cause of the shell shock see, all the noise of the guns, did 'is 'ead in. Me da bought 'im fer a

shillin', otherwise it would've bin the knacker's yard, like so many others. 'Ee was an army
grai, a kushti grai.

Me da thought the world of 'im and took 'im everywhere. The chavies loved 'im and 'ee
them. The only time 'ee stood still was when they were strokin' 'im. *'Ain't you a luvley boy?'*
They'd say. Me da sold 'errin's in the main square and Mad Alf would trot to and fro until it
was time to go 'ome. I was only a nipper but I remember it well. Me da comin' back to the
vardo, tellin' us about 'is day, stinkin' of fish.

'Ee used to let me give Mad Alf some 'obben, carrots and grains and all the time 'ee kept
'oppin' from one foot to the other, 'ee was beautiful though. When we settled fer the raddi,
we'd 'ear a strange noise, a sort of screechin' sound, 'igh pitched. Da said *'Ee's 'ad it ard,*
'ee done 'is bit.' *'Ee must of bin frit to death, going didilow on the battlefield'* me da said,
then 'ee tutted and put 'is 'ead down so I couldn't see the tears.

One day I 'eard someone cryin', I went outside and saw me dad on the ground, is 'ead bent
down, one vast on the grai's neck, the 'uver on 'is back. Mad Alf lie mullered. The first time
I ever saw a mullered grai. No words fer it.

Da made a wooden carvin' of Mad Alf which took pride of place on the mantle piece. 'Ee
couldn't spell but 'ee managed to write, 'Ere is Mad Alf, our phral, a kushti grai. Duvel Parik
me freno.

Romani words: Kushti − lovely; Grai − horse; Chavies − children; Vardo − wagon; Hobben − food; Raddi − night; Didilow − out of his mind; Vast − hand; Mullered − dead; Phral: brother/best mate; Duvel parik me freno: God bless my friend.

Like Raine, Damian has witnessed the special connection formed between Travellers and their horses, a connection he has experienced himself at the horse fairs he has attended over the years. He recounts spending time mucking out and brushing, feeding and watering the horses as a child. 'I used to spend time with them whenever I could. It calmed me down.' Like many of us, Damian believes humans and horses share a special bond, not wanting things from us in the way people do, and seeming to enjoy human company, even when, as Damian points out, they know you have nothing to offer besides a few words of Romani and a pat on the side of the neck. 'Sometimes I feel like they've got more faith in us than we've got in ourselves. And I think that's part of the reason I love to be around them. They remind me of who I really am and that there's no point running away from it.'

U

The image of Travellers trotting their vardos through the hills and meadows of Britain dates back long before the First and Second World Wars, originating instead from the 'wagon years', the heyday of nomadic, untethered living that brought Traveller communities through the 1800s and into the early twentieth century. Before this, the history of Traveller people is not entirely clear, partly because they passed down their stories orally, generation to generation, and historically preferred to keep those stories within their own communities. Although originally thought to have come from Egypt – a sixteenth-century theory that first mutated the word 'Egyptian' into 'Gypsy' – genetic analysis actually suggests that a large portion of Travellers arrived in a single wave from the north-west of India around 1,500 years ago. By the time they arrived in Spain, around the fifteenth century, known for their exotic music, dancing and skill with horses, they were accompanied by a legend that they had been expelled from Egypt for trying to hide Jesus. But Travellers were also faced with endless attempts to expel or imprison them, a persecution that has plagued Traveller culture ever since. Centuries of discrimination has kept many of them marginalised, and in the twentieth century, fascist regimes also implemented the systematic extermination of Travellers in their thousands. Historians estimate that between 200,000 and 500,000 Roma and Sinti people (a subgroup of Romani people mostly found in Germany) were murdered by the Nazis and their collaborators. Many more were imprisoned, used as forced labour or subjected to forced sterilisation and medical experimentation. This period of genocide made such a mark on Traveller culture, it has its own Romani name – *Porajmos*, or 'the Devouring'.

Most of what remains of the wagon years was immortalised either in music, folktales and oral stories, or in the art and literature of the time, depicting the lives of the Travellers and their families. Within this iconography, the vardo wagon has become one of the most recognisable symbols of Traveller culture, even today, despite not having been in common use for more than a century. It is through the Traveller's vardo that we find the most romanticised (and perhaps the most empathetic) interpretation of Traveller life. One of nomadic freedom, strong will and independence, of romance and fierce family bonds, of a deep, ancient connection with the landscape, of fortune telling, curses, magic and mischief, and of the rural industries that employed Traveller people throughout the seasons, drawing them from place to place with each bud and fall of the leaf. Another of Raine Geoghegan's poems captures the seasonality of life in the vardo, particularly around springtime when the Earth would be stirring and the *koring chiriclo*, the cuckoo, would start calling:

'Koring Chiriclo II – a triolet'

Jel on me dad would say.
Pack up yer covels, we'll be on our way.
Take our time, get to Frome's 'ill by May.
Jel on, me dad would say.
The cuckoo's callin', untie the grai,
up onto the vardo. It's a kushti day.
Jel on, me dad would say.
Pack up yer covels. We'll be on our way.

Romani words: Koring chiriclo – the cuckoo; Jel on – move on; Covels –
belongings; Grai – horses; Vardo – wagon; Kushti – lovely.

With its large wheels, bow-topped or wooden roofs, cast
iron cooking stove, chimney, built-in furniture and sleeping
bunks, it's no wonder the vardo still retains the romanticised,
cosy charm that once kept Travellers safe and warm on the
road. A quick search on Airbnb reveals hundreds of 'Gypsy
Caravan'-style accommodation choices, complete with fire
pits beneath glittering night skies – everything you need to
channel your inner nature-loving nomad. But beyond the
physical structure of the vardo, it was their designs that
arguably made these wagons the most striking. The
woodwork was, traditionally, exceptional, with elaborately
carved designs painted with ornate colours and motifs, such
as drawings of horses, dogs, birds, lions, gryphons, flowers
and vines. Gold leaf was used to accentuate the most
beautiful details, and the wealth of the vardo and its family
was often reflected in these paintings. Perhaps one of the
most famous examples of this paintwork – albeit one of the
most appropriated – was on John Lennon's 1965 Rolls
Royce Phantom V Limousine, which he commissioned to
have designed in 'Romani style' colours and motifs. It
features swirls of bright orange, red and blue, floral designs
inspired by dahlias and delphiniums and a giant Libra
symbol painted on the top (Lennon's astrological sign). It is

now on display in the Royal BC Museum in British Columbia, Canada.

Closer to home, and held within the collection of another museum, one Travellers' vardo has been on display to the general public since 1953. It was originally displayed outside Blaise Museum in Bristol, a facility formerly specialising in folk history, but was moved to Bristol Museum & Art Gallery four years later, where it has remained ever since. As an undergraduate living in Bristol, I remember visiting the vardo and immediately choosing it as my favourite piece in the museum, tucked away in a corner but still resplendent in colour and character. And although an artefact on permanent display indoors might seem like the antithesis of the Traveller 'spirit', it is still bringing Traveller communities together generations after it was first donated to the museum. Some of the earliest people known to have lived in the vardo were Noah and Annie O'Connor, who travelled with their family from around 1916 until Noah was killed in a road accident in 1925. The family then downsized and the vardo was moved to Lock's Yard Caravan Park in Bedminster, before eventually being sold to a holiday camp in Glamorgan in 1951. Since its arrival in the museum, members of the O'Connor family have visited the vardo several times, sharing further memories with the museum staff and donating personal family items, including a horse whip, neckerchief, photos and a set of cooking pots.

The vardo may have been a vital part of Traveller life during the wagon years, but what about the horses who pulled them? Enter the Gypsy cob, also known as the Irish cob, galineers cob or gypsy vanner, a small but solid breed of horse originating from the UK and Ireland. Known for their decadent feathered feet, and often decorated with piebald or skewbald colouring (piebald is blotched with white and black; skewbald is blotched with white and any colour other than black), some claim the Gypsy cobs were bred with two aims in mind: to pull the vardo with ease, and to have a gentle nature for the children. During the First World War, it was said that the British Army avoided conscripting coloured horses as they were too easily spotted on the battlefield. Many Travellers capitalised on this, breeding hundreds of colourful horses to pull their wagons, and their colourful coats soon became a status symbol; the flashier the cob, the more valuable they became – and the harder they were to steal! By the time the wagon years came to an end, the Gypsy cob had become such an iconic figure in Traveller communities that even when they were no longer required to pull the vardos, they were still cared for, kept and sold en masse by those who saw the beauty in their form. Even today, cobs made up the majority of horses I saw being traded and paraded at the Wickham Horse Fair, and it was refreshing to see these gentle, stocky animals being valued so highly in a world of thoroughbreds, Dutch warmbloods and Arabs.

But the horses were, of course, only one part of the story. For Damian Le Bas, horse fairs like Appleby and Wickham are some of the most important fixtures in the Traveller year. 'Infinitely important, really,' he explained, 'since they're one of the main ways the culture has of encountering itself. You'd expect them to be important based on the role of the horse, as I've said, but it's more than that. And it's more than the fact that you can often buy Travellers' wares at a fair that are really hard to find elsewhere. Things like stainless steel water containers built for the road, or Crown Derby china sets. A horse fair is the only time you can visit a public space, as an ethnic Gypsy or Traveller, and have your ethnicity be in the majority. Where you can pass by someone in the street and hear them speaking your ancestral language, whether that's Romani or the Gamin [also known as Shelta] or the Beurla-Reagaird [a near-extinct Scottish, Gaelic-based language]. Normally we only get to speak our language within the family, so it is an incredibly powerful feeling, especially if you're used to being an unwelcome presence on the fringe of the community, on a site in a village that has been protested against by your neighbours, or on a council-run Traveller site on the edge of town that taxi drivers refuse to take passengers to. These sort of experiences are very common for Gypsies and Travellers, so to be able to turn up somewhere, to be able to "strut your stuff" in a way, to feel like it's fine and maybe even glamorous to be one of us, rather than an unwanted presence, just for a day or two every year, is to be reminded that you're part of something bigger. That it has survived, and that there is not just continuity, but also change.'

Travellers have always been faced with – and adapted to – change: the change of scene as they moved from place to place, county to county, and the changes in law that have stripped them of their rights and further marginalised them to the fringes of society. The Inclosure Acts between 1604 and 1914, for example, sealed off almost seven million acres of common land and gave it to private landowners, changing the lives of rural people and Travellers for the worse – and yet they adapted. In 1960, a new Caravan Sites and Control of Development Act gave local authorities even more power to close the commons to Travellers, while rarely utilising the powers granted within the same Act to open new caravan sites to compensate for the losses. Today, the majority of Travellers continue to experience discrimination in their daily lives; one 2017 survey found that 91 per cent of Traveller respondents had experienced discrimination and 77 per cent had experienced hate speech or been the victim of a hate crime.

Despite the difficulties they face, however, they continue to swim through the tide of change. And for Damian, change can be positive, even within the ancient setting of the old horse fairs. 'There is incremental change every year,' he observed. 'New children born, new fashions, new music. And new relationships. Less so these days, but still the case is that lots of Travellers meet their future spouses at horse fairs.

When you're a scattered people, numerically small, spread all over an archipelago with thousands of islands like the British Isles, it's mind-blowing to be able to turn up somewhere and be temporarily united. So many communities have their equivalents to this. Pilgrimages, they are often called. It's why people made the journey from the Orkney islands to Stonehenge in ancient times. It was a hell of a journey, but worth it. Of course, not everyone who lives in a place that hosts a Travellers' fair is as thrilled about the fair thing as I am, but that's another question. Ultimately, we've got as much right to the land as anyone else. And a lot of the dislike of fairs is as much a class prejudice as an ethnic one, with well-to-do people unhappy to see people who aren't like them enjoying an outdoor space. I can sympathise when people have had negative experiences with Traveller groups or individuals, but I can't empathise with an attitude based on discrimination.'

As for the horses with whom Travellers have shared the open road for so many centuries, I asked Damian whether he saw a future for them in our increasingly mechanised society. 'I don't know if they'll always play the same role,' he said. 'But I reckon as long as there are Travellers, there'll be Travellers who have horses. The vast majority of Travellers who have horses don't need them any more in any material sense of dire need, but then how do you define "need"? If having a horse keeps you happy, maybe it even keeps you sane to get out on your horse and away from the stresses of life, to have that relationship with a horse, with a time when things were different and when life had a different pace, is that not a genuine need? If going out with the sulky on a weekend reminds you of your mother and father who used to do that years ago, and is therefore a form of commemoration, a sort of ritual of remembrance as well as a recreation, is that not culturally noble, and worthy of preservation for its own sake? Travellers don't often articulate this stuff explicitly but I think we all think about it. It's why we're so stubborn when it comes to horses. Why we don't really care whether other people think we should give them up, because we know there's something about them they just don't understand. I'm sure everyone who rides and who keeps horses feels basically the same way about it. One person's pragmatism is another person's soulless approach to life. And who knows? The horse might make a comeback on a bigger scale as the availability of energy changes and as people make adaptations. You can see this happening now, in places. But it could become a more normal thing, to see people who have "gone backwards" in order to move forwards.'

The sky above Wickham darkened through the morning until thick drops of rain broke through and showered the central running track. But it made no difference; the Travellers continued on in defiance, their eyes glittering with the resilience that comes from a centuries-old collective sense of outsider identity. I took a photograph of a girl in her late teens riding a black-and-white cob bareback, cigarette in one hand, reins in the other. She looked powerful as she rode slowly through the crowded lanes, weaving between spectators, handlers, and the large number of police and animal welfare officers standing by. The police seemed friendly enough; they told us days like these could go completely smoothly, or turn in a split-second. They stood along the running track and watched the horses pass by, quietly interested in the proceedings. The animal welfare officers told me that, contrary to popular belief, the animals at Traveller fairs were usually well cared for, and their handlers were more often than not open to conversations with the welfare team about how they could improve the daily lives of their horses.

I stayed until the rain cleared and the sun began to shine through the clouds. Walking away from the edge of the running track, along which a group of young, tweed-clad boys were now enthusiastically trotting a pony, I made my way back through the ghost town of Wickham, the sights and sounds of its closed cafés and antique shops replaced by the aroma of candy floss and horse manure, and the *whirr-clink* of the fairground rides. Centuries of Travellers coming together in the name of horsemanship and community; the beat of horses' feet against tarmacked roads, the murmur of an ancient tongue, the chime of the carousel spinning round and round. Who knew how many more horse fairs this quiet Hampshire village would witness in the years to come?

CHAPTER EIGHT

Beasts of Burden

A fresh Sunday morning in October, and I could hear church bells pealing in the town square. Dave had taken Olive down to the park to burn off some of that early morning one-year-old energy, and I sat alone sipping coffee, savouring half an hour of peace and stillness. I was watching a male blackbird, still flecked with the chestnut feathers of youth, rooting through the debris beneath the buddleia in our front garden. Dead moss and leaves, scaffold planks and a broken paving stone; a sanctuary for insects frequented by little brown birds. Not a natural gardener, I'd neglected pruning the buddleia for the last two years and the stems stretched up to the autumn sky, the remnants of this year's blossoms turning dull and brittle as I watched, sleepy-eyed, and listened to the bells.

The first bells to ring in British churches arrived from 400AD, brought over by monks and friars coming to join religious orders. Being one of the loudest musical instruments in the world, a ringing bell can be heard for many miles over land and sea. On this slow autumn morning, the bells tumbled through the air like skylark song. There is something comforting in the sound that has little to do with religion, something ageless and uncomplicated. Once they would have called people to worship or brought workers in from the fields, farmers with their heavy horses plodding over the hills. In European traditions, a ringing bell was thought to ward off storms brewed by the devil, as described in the inscription on a bell in the Church of Santa Maria degli Angioli in Lugano, Switzerland: 'The sound of this bell vanquishes tempests, repels demons, and summons men.' There were, thankfully, no demons running around my cul-de-sac this morning;

only red maple leaves melting into the earth, a loaf-shaped cat beneath the pyracantha and the lingering scent of coffee. I drained the cup and went to get dressed. Today I would need my wellies because this afternoon, we were off to a ploughing match.

First introduced to the British Isles in 1066, the draught horse, commonly known as the heavy horse, takes its name from the Old English word *dragan*, which means to haul or draw. Before the development of the internal combustion engine in the nineteenth century, heavy horses were an essential source of power on land, transporting goods up and down the country, grinding malt for beer, pulling canal boats, hauling artillery and ploughing the land. But after the Second World War, the mechanisation of farming saw a decline in heavy horses working on farms and in breweries. No longer able to compete with the speed and power of tractors and other machinery, over the last few decades the number of heavy horses in the British Isles has dwindled to only a few thousand individuals across a handful of breeds, including the traditional 'native' Shire, Clydesdale, British Percheron and Suffolk Punch horses. Those that remain are treasured for their gentle nature and their embodiment of the British rural identity, and fortunately, you rarely need to travel far to see them up close.

There was a satisfying crunch underfoot as I stepped out of the car and stamped down onto stubble. Sunlight slipped through a light wash of cloud, and I could smell the distant sea on the wind. We had come to a ploughing match and country fair in Droxford, a village on the western edge of the South Downs National Park once inhabited by Nordic tribes. It is a beautiful and secluded area — so secluded, in fact, that it was chosen by Winston Churchill as a meeting place in the lead up to D-Day. Just days before the invasion took place, Churchill brought together his war cabinet, including world leaders from the United States, France, Canada and South Africa, on an armoured train at the old Droxford Station on the now defunct Meon Valley railway line. Not only was Droxford close to a number of Allied troops who were based in the area ahead of the invasion, but it was hoped the secluded location in deep, leafy woodland would mean that news of the meeting would avoid reaching German ears. It was easy to see why such a place was chosen, even today, 80 years after it all happened. We were miles from anywhere, surrounded only by trees and fields, expensive cars and pretty buildings, including a sixteenth-century coaching inn called the White Horse.

The aim of a ploughing match is for a person and their horse (there are also classes for tractor ploughing) to plough part of a field, with points awarded for straightness and neatness of the resulting furrows. We made our way past the match fields en route to the coffee shack, and stopped to watch the heavy horses in motion. Each plough was pulled by two horses and balanced by a man at the back, with an extra person on hand to guide at the front if needed. It seemed, from our viewpoint, far more strenuous for the humans involved than the horses, with one unfortunate ploughman falling face-first into the soil after a particularly hefty jerk of the plough. The horses themselves were feather-footed giants, coats shining in the October light and their manes snaked with ribbons. The commentator told us over the speaker that dried raffia palms would have traditionally been woven into their manes for decoration, along with the brass plaques that dangled from the horses' tack, clinking with every step through the thick mud clods.

Seven hundred miles north of this ploughing match, another one takes place every year on the Orcadian island of South Ronaldsay – although there's something a little different about the horses they use. This match is thought to date back at least 200 years, if not more; the earliest

ploughs were made of ox hooves or horns tied to a stick,
until 1920 when the first miniature metal plough was
forged by the local blacksmith. Today, similar ploughs are
still polished, the harnesses' buttons cleaned and the ribbons
replaced − but it isn't the traditional Clydesdale that is
tacked up with it all. Instead, the boys and girls of South
Ronaldsay are the competitors. The boys plough the four-
foot square patch they are given on the hard flats of the
Sands O'Wright, with the timing of the contest worked
around the turning of the tides. Meanwhile, the girls dress
as the draught horses and parade around, complete with a
collar, hat, belt and feet decorations made of baubles, pom-
poms and fringes to mimic the hoof feathers. While
originally only the boys were allowed to participate, it was
later decided that girls could take part, too − but only in the
role of the horse.

The longevity of this tradition, and the existence of the
match we were at today, demonstrates how horse-drawn
ploughing still has a strong fan base of people who are
passionate about more traditional ways of working with the
land. Although it has not been in common use since the
advent of mechanised agriculture, there are advantages to
the practice, according to the Society of Ploughmen. Horse-
drawn ploughing is thought to effectively invert the soil,
control weeds, improve drainage, aerate and improve the soil
structure, and reduce the risk of disease. A recent study by
the United Nations suggests that around one third of the
Earth's land is classed as severely degraded, with fertile soil
being lost at a rate of 24 billion tonnes per year globally.
Horse-drawn ploughing may not be a viable solution to all
the world's soil issues, but to see these animals here, so gently
and carefully moving the earth from one space to another, it
is easy to remember there were once alternative, more
harmonious ways to exist. So often the solutions to our
problems lie behind us, just as the plough, in the horse's
wake, reveals fresh soil to the autumn sun.

We admired the horses ploughing for a while longer, plodding through the fields in gentle waves, to and fro, up and down. I took one of my dogs, Pablo, to register for the Handsomest Dog category in the dog show (which, criminally, he did not win), and while we waited, I watched a side-saddle display in the main arena. Ladies in tweed habits with netted faces, hair slicked back into flawless buns under perfectly positioned hats – standards of neatness I could never dream of achieving. One rider carried a cane in her right hand, which acted like another leg to make up for the fact that both of hers were slung to the left of her horse's mane. It looked difficult from down on the ground, but the commentator assured the crowd that the shoulders were still above the hips, square-on to the horse, which meant, with a little practice, any rider could adjust to it.

I watched the ladies riding until it was time to sign Pablo up for his dog show debut, making a mental note to try side-saddle if ever offered the chance. It was heartening to see these traditions kept alive with such passion and dedication, and one of the reasons I found these country shows so enjoyable. The grace of the side-saddlers like a scene from *Downton Abbey*; the chink of a blacksmith forging a horseshoe; the heavy horses gleaming in the afternoon sun. Not even the smell of fried food or the drab jingle of a gaudy carousel could shatter the charm of nostalgia about the place. And yet, there was something about these huge, powerful horses that belonged not in the past, but in an imagined future. Here was a forgotten, more humble source of energy, a gentler idea of what it means to be productive. An animal that still has a role to play in the working world, and one that might even help us live more harmoniously with the land.

There are far fewer working horses in the UK than there were a century ago, but that doesn't mean they have disappeared completely. Heavy horses can still be found working the land on farms, smallholdings and in market gardens, where they are particularly suited to harrowing, rolling, cultivating and carting, in addition to carrying winter feed out to other livestock, maintaining pasture, hoeing between vegetable rows and moving heavy objects around. Working horses are also used for demonstrations in heritage centres like the Weald & Downland Museum in Sussex, as well as boosting tourism with horse-drawn canal holidays, 'Gypsy' caravan experiences and horse-and-cart rides.

But it is the sheer muscular power of the heavy horse that makes these animals so mesmerising to watch. When demand grew for horses that could work fields and pull heavy loads, breeders began to produce stronger horses to meet that demand. Today, the strongest heavy horse is thought to be the American Belgian. These gentle giants stand up to 18 hands (1.8m) tall and weigh up to 900kg, and were originally bred as warhorses before transitioning to farm work. In the UK, the Shire horse is often considered the strongest native breed; in 1924, a Shire set the record for the most weight ever pulled by a horse with a load weighing an incredible 26 tonnes. One of the oldest heavy horse breeds in England, they were also once used as warhorses to haul artillery, although today they are better known for their calm and gentle nature.

Even the smallest heavy horses are powerful creatures. In Herefordshire's Golden Valley, a wild, untamed landscape speckled with ancient monuments, churches, ruined castles, mountains and rivers, there is a seventeenth-century stone mill called Fair Oak still in operation, worked by a Gypsy cob named Tommy. For 300 years, almost every farm in Herefordshire would have cultivated their own apple orchards and built their own mills to make cider as part payment for their workers. They were even known to avoid paying an 'orchard tax' by planting apple trees in the public hedgerows, collecting the apples up every autumn and carting them back to the farm. The cider-making process was a collaborative effort, with workers and other locals joining in to gather and prepare the apples for the mill, where they would be pulped by horsepower, squeezed and fermented.

Orchards have been used to grow food in Britain for thousands of years. There were once countless apple cultivars in a huge range of colours, sizes and flavours. Many orchards can still be found around western and south-western counties, as well as in Norfolk, Suffolk, Kent and Sussex. Not only are they useful and beautiful spaces, they are also great for pollinators who thrive on the rotten fruit and deadwood habitats. A late summer evening in an English orchard is alive with the hum of bees and hornets feasting on fallen fruits that melt, oozing, into the grass. Traditional cider apples were more closely related to the wild crab apple than sweeter eating or cooking apples; small, hard and often heavily blotched, they were also high in the bitter tannins that made them perfect for cider but a horrible choice for a snack. Due to this diversity in tannins, apple specialists, known as pomologists, divide cider apples into bittersweets and bittersharps, depending on their flavour.

Because they were destined to be milled, cider apples didn't need to look pretty, so it was usual to harvest them by knocking them off the trees using ash poles up to five metres long, sometimes fitted with iron hooks to shake the branches. In Herefordshire, the fruit was then gathered into heaps, called *tumps*, and left in the orchard for two to three weeks before milling, covered in straw. This helped reduce some of the moisture content and concentrate the sugars in the juice, mellowing the flavour. Herefordshire, Gloucestershire and Worcestershire were also known for their perry cider, made using pear cultivars with beautiful and amusing names like the Bosbury Scarlet, Stinking Bishop and Merrylegs (the latter named for its effect on the drinker). Pear trees have since become a distinctive feature of the landscape around these counties, growing more than 15m tall, often with an elegant curving crown at the top. They also live much longer than apple trees, with some specimens still bearing fruit at 200 years old.

When the fruit had softened on the orchard floor, it was ready to be taken to the cider mill, first to be pulped and then to press out the juice. Around 50kg of fruit was laid on the central pier of the mill before harnessing up the horse, whose job it was to crush the fruit using a vertical grindstone. The cidermaker would walk behind the horse, knocking apples into the bed of the mill as they went until it was full of pulped fruit, which turned deep brown and aromatic as it was exposed to the air. Once the pulp was milled, it was packed into horsehair cloths known as *hairs* and pressed; the juice was then taken away for fermentation. A beautifully preserved example of a horse-powered cider press can be found in Buckland Abbey, former home of Sir Francis Drake and now in the care of the National Trust, in Devon. Traditional cider was often incredibly sharp and acidic, as almost all the sugar was fermented out to alcohol. In fact, it had sometimes already started going off by the time it was consumed, which gave the cider a reputation for being extremely sour and strong, said to have a delayed effect 'like the kick of a mad horse'. This is what became known as scrumpy, or 'squeal-pig' cider in Herefordshire, because that was the noise someone might make if they tasted it by accident.

During the Victorian era, with the invention of the portable mill and improved press design, cidermakers began to take their craft on the road, travelling between counties and processing the apples of other orchards. The maker's equipment would be towed from farm to farm by a team of horses, and on reaching their destination, a yoke would be fitted to the top of the mill so the horse could power it by walking in a circular path around the mill. In Thomas Hardy's novel *The Woodlanders*, the protagonist Giles

Winterborne is a travelling cidermaker who spends each autumn moving from village to village with his horses, mill and press. Nobody describes a rural landscape quite like Hardy, who makes it so easy to imagine that sensation of slow decay in the harvest air, the hum of fermenting apples, the glow of the autumn sun and the scent of the warm horse plodding round and round and round.

When the First World War broke out, many farm workers were called up to fight, and the horses that powered the mills were phased out and replaced by tractors. Fair Oak, too, succumbed to the change, so that by 2010, the stone mill had been neglected for almost a century. The huge, hand-carved millstone was miraculously still intact, but other pieces were broken and the facility was unusable. Then, in 2011, a local group decided to restore the mill back to working order, and use it once again to produce cider. With no real reference guide or proper instructions, the group managed to fix the broken mechanisms and find a Gypsy cob stallion called Pye to power the millstone. As the first apples were crushed after decades of disuse, Fair Oak became potentially the only horse-drawn mill in the country to once again operate as a commercial cider producer.

To make a decent quantity of cider, the Fair Oak team source apple cultivars from around the Golden Valley, including classic varieties like the Foxwell, Yarlington Mill, Dabinett and Kingston Black. Most of these apples are donated by local orchard keepers in exchange for the cider they go on to produce. Inside the mill, a cobbled floor is dappled by the hooves of countless horses over the centuries and today's star of the mill is a Gypsy cob called Tommy. A harness is hung around the horse's neck and shoulders, which enables him to walk in a slow circle, rolling a large stone and crushing the apples as he goes. With no artificial ingredients added and different apples used year on year, depending on the weather, this might be as close as we can get to the authentic Herefordshire cider that shaped this landscape for so many centuries, powered by a single, gentle horse, patiently pacing to the grind of his own millstone.

♘

The road from South Harting to Lavant was strewn with trees on the morning I drove over the Hampshire border and into Sussex. In the week prior, the UK had been thrown into three consecutive storms, Dudley, Eunice and Franklin, and the weather was still blustery enough that plenty of trees remained uprooted or fallen. One of them took up an entire lane of the single carriageway, and I was forced to sweep around the traffic cones and drive on the wrong side of the road for a few uncomfortable seconds. Despite occasional post-storm hazards, however, I felt relaxed at the wheel. This was one of my favourite roads in the South Downs, an eight-mile stretch that brought back memories of my driving lessons to Chichester and back – I was taught to drive by an instructor who taught the army how to drive tanks; needless to say, he was very efficient. One evening, exhausted after two hours spent tackling roundabouts, I remembered how a barn owl had flown low in front of us on the road and disappeared into the trees. This was a road of treasures, winding over the wildflower carpets of Harting Down and around green folds of meadow and farmland. In summer, it was speckled with classic cars on their way to Goodwood Racecourse; in winter, the yew trees of Kingley Vale grew black against the bare woods. And a few miles further along the road, in a professional textile studio in the village of West Dean, the final tapestry was woven for Stirling Castle's 'Hunt of the Unicorn' recreation project.

This morning, however, I was destined for none of these fascinating places. Instead, I parked at the Weald & Downland Living Museum in the village of Singleton, a 40-acre open-air museum filled with more than 50 historic buildings dating back to the Anglo-Saxons, as well as rustic gardens, livestock, mixed woodland and a mill pond. This was not my first visit to the museum; in fact, I had long considered this one of my 'happy places' – somewhere peaceful and inspiring, full of passionate staff and volunteers, infinite historical details, and delicious cake and coffee. It was also the chosen setting for BBC One's *The Repair Shop*, in which family heirlooms are restored for their owners, although it was not Jay Blades I had come to meet today.

I parked the car and wandered down to meet Josh, one of the marketing team who had kindly agreed to introduce me to the museum's working animals supervisor, Andy, and a gelding (a castrated male horse) called Ollie. Andy and Ollie were getting ready for a day's work around the museum where a total of three horses carry out traditional farming tasks throughout the year, including pulling carts, cutting hay and ploughing. Ollie is an eight-year-old Percheron, a breed originating from the Huisne river valley in western France, once part of the former Perche province that gave the breed its name. Their amenability, elegance and willingness to work have made them a popular draught horse, and Ollie had been working at the museum since he graduated from training four years before. With the museum's two other resident Percherons, Leon and Kash, I watched Ollie complete a ploughing challenge led by Andy, who was now tacking him up in the stable courtyard. Keen to deepen his knowledge of traditional farming practices, Andy and his horses managed to plough 12 acres of land in only 15 days using traditional methods, working through all weathers for more than 100 hours. Now well-rested and back to work, Ollie stood relaxed and calm in front of me while Andy prepared him for the day, as the sun broke through the February clouds warming us through.

To choose a career with horses, Andy told me, is to choose a life on minimum wage; I laughed and said that was the same for writers. But if equine life *is* the one for you, how on earth do you make it work? And, even more intriguing, how

does one end up with a job caring for three beautiful horses
in an open-air museum in Sussex, ploughing fields, carting
timber and educating the visitors about the history of rural
life? Andy's story started in an unexpected place. He was not
from a 'horsey' background, but instead grew up in a low-
income household on a council estate in Exmoor in Devon.
Despite not riding his first horse until he was aged 19, Andy
was always drawn to the enchantment of the countryside
and the connection forged between humans and horses. As
soon as he was old enough to work, he used his wages to
pay for riding lessons, during which he learned to ride polo
ponies (a baptism of fire, if ever there was one). Within four
months, Andy had secured his first job working with the
free-roaming ponies on Exmoor. Having no fear of horses
or outdoor work helped him embrace such an unconventional
career. Even so, he knew he would have to find a way to
make his chosen path financially viable. Keen to find his
niche, Andy soon learned to 'drive' horses before turning his
attention to heavy horses. When he was finally taken on as
an apprentice for a local farmer that still used horses to work
the land, Andy told me it felt like coming home. That was 10
years ago, and for the last three years, he had been working at
Singleton. The secret to Andy's success? He was utterly
dedicated to his craft and passionate about the animals he
worked with, but he assured me he was also blessed with
good luck. Looking around at the place Andy called work
and home (he lived on site with his partner), I could imagine
he felt fortunate waking up to this every day.

I followed Andy, Ollie and their small team of staff along
the track, over a grassy slope and up into the woods. Ollie
was harnessed to a small metal cart ready for loading with
brushwood, which would then be taken down to the
bakehouse and used in the ovens; the large surface area of a
brushwood bundle ensured a hot flame, which was ideal for
baking bread. This year, the horses were being used to grow
a dredge corn of oats and peas, as well as spelt, a type of

wheat that has been cultivated since around 5000BC. The staff were unable to use their heritage wheat crops to make bread for human consumption at the museum, as the testing, cleaning and general health and safety required was logistically impractical. Instead, they used their crops to feed the horses, as well as the geese, chickens and ducks. A good crop provided straw for thatch or bedding, if the quality was poorer. The oats and peas would be cut green and fed to the horses as hay, and a summer cover crop would also be sown to plough back into the earth to manage soil erosion and increase fertility. In winter, a crop of roots would be harvested to feed the sheep, whose droppings would continue to fertilise the soil, ready for the next season. It was an intricate process based on Victorian and Edwardian farming calendars, and one that relied entirely on Andy and his horses' connection with the rhythms and cycles of the year.

The woodland floor was strewn with twigs and branches from last week's storms, as well as brittle leaves and beech mast left over from the autumn. Curled and crushed underfoot, they would quietly dissolve into the soil and sprout up again anew; a sapling or a wildflower, made out of nothing but old trees and air and water. The chalk track was slippery, and I could see hoofprints dug into the ground where Ollie had slid slightly, before righting himself and moving on up the hill. The rain had cleared, and although as cold as it was likely to be on a February morning, the sun poured down through the gaps in the trees and lit everything up, casting a warm and fragrant spell over the woodland. A buzzard mewed somewhere, and green buds were already swelling at the tips of tree limbs. Onwards the wheel turned, ever onwards.

Like everything else at the Weald & Downland Museum, Ollie's harness was as historically accurate as possible, although Andy pointed out where some allowances had been made for the sake of his welfare and comfort. All the horses at the museum wore a Scandinavian-made timber harness that was around 90 per cent historically correct; it worked in the same way as the older versions, but they were put together differently, just as old and new cars, at their heart, still share the same old combustion engine technology. Andy mentioned that it was communities like the Amish and Old Order Mennonites who were responsible for some of the modern improvements to draught horse equipment, as they do not use tractors or machines to pull their fields and rely on horsepower to pull ploughs and other farm equipment. Although their beliefs are centred on simple living, strong faith and community, they still need to treat their farms like a business to secure a sustainable lifestyle, which means they are able to find ways to make life more efficient without straying from their core values. Their farming model has attracted so much attention around the world that a movement has formed to show how horsepower can help kickstart new farming businesses without the need for huge amounts of wealth. A single new tractor can cost six figures – an impossible amount for someone starting out on their own. But as Andy pointed out, if you are open to working with horses and willing to fully commit to the project for a few years, many believe it is possible to build up a small but successful farming practice that could then qualify for a larger financial backing.

But it isn't only for economic reasons that horse-drawn farming still intrigues so many. The agricultural landscape changed dramatically after the end of the Second World War, when a push for profit and productivity gave rise to intensive farming. The small- and medium-sized mixed farms that once speckled the English landscape were replaced by large-scale commercial farms, dependent on powerful machinery, fertilisers and synthetic pesticides. Production rocketed and prices dropped, but at a huge cost to human, animal and environmental health. Today, more and more members of the farming community are keen to find ways to return to a less damaging way of managing the land, while still ensuring a secure supply of affordable food. And while we're unlikely to find all our tractors and combine harvesters soon replaced with heavy horses, Andy pointed out to me how much more aligned with the landscape this non-mechanical way of farming can be. Without the need to force something out of every inch of land and hour of time, there is more room for wildlife to breathe – and to thrive. In keeping with the museum's ethos, Andy usually farms without electric lighting, which means he is forced to adapt to the rhythms and seasons of the year, stopping when it gets dark or when the weather requires it – or simply when he or the horse are too tired to carry on. You can't pour petrol into a horse to get him moving again, which means Andy must play the long game; non-mechanical farming is labour intensive, and every minute of work is a load of energy burned. He does as much as he needs to do and no more, and this is where Andy's practice tends to diverge from a more intensive approach. Instead of squeezing out everything he can from the land, he takes only what he needs – and leaves the rest. It is a beautiful concept, and one that could easily be dismissed as fantasy if we cannot open our minds to it. But as Andy pointed out, it is perfectly possible to be an agricultural nation and nurture our wildlife at the same time. And why does he believe that? Because, aside from the last few decades, we've been doing it for hundreds of years. In fact, our entire country was built on it.

Horsepower is not only useful in the farming world. A hundred miles west of the Weald & Downland Museum, further along the south coast, one Dorset-based industry is thriving on a much larger scale than the museum's woods and fields. Based in Corfe Castle, Toby Hoad and his team at Dorset Horse Logging specialise in felling and low-impact timber extraction using heavy horses. In doing so, they provide a safe, efficient and environmentally conscious service, while also being commercially viable. There are many benefits of horse-powered timber extraction, but one of the most important is being able to work with minimal disturbance to woodland floors and pathways, leaving fewer of the marks usually made by heavy machinery. In fact, the light scarification of the ground often creates seed beds for natural regeneration. The horses are also able to work safely on steep slopes and access narrower paths and gateways, as well as reducing accidental tree damage, excess noise and air pollution. It wasn't long ago that this kind of timber extraction still dominated parts of the British landscape, including areas with high rainfall in the north and west. In December 1917, the Timber Supplies Department in England and Wales owned 587 horses and hired many more, as well as using horse-operated tramways. Even by the 1960s, horses still provided the dominant means of extraction in the hill countries, particularly in the Pennines, North York Moors, Lake District and Shropshire Hills; records suggest there were around 396 horses still in use by the Forestry Commission in England, Scotland and Wales, compared to around 350 tractors. Flash forward to twenty-first-century southern England, and Toby and his horses continue to be in high demand, proving that horses still play a vital role in landscape management. 'There is a place for machinery in forestry,' he agrees. 'But on a smaller scale – with our low impact, sensitive sites – this just works perfectly.'

Back at the museum, I watched the team pack brushwood onto the cart. They were harvested from the coppiced areas of the woodland, where it wasn't only the traditional hazel trees that were grown and coppiced, but anything that could be used for firewood; this was closer to the old days, when the decline of the coal industry saw a resurgence in burning firewood as fuel. Coppicing is a woodland management technique that dates back to the Stone Age, through which trees are repeatedly felled and allowed to grow back again to provide a sustainable supply of timber. The practice has huge benefits for wildlife and, as the trees' root systems are already established, regrowth is quick and less susceptible to animal browsing or being shaded out by taller trees. Once cut, the wood was usually processed here in the woods to save the horses carting entire trees down to the farm. Efficiency, as always, was key.

I followed Ollie and his team of humans back down the track, his cart loaded up with bundles that brushed the edges of the trees as we moved through the woods to the main site. Like many horse breeds, a healthy Percheron would be expected to live well into their twenties. They don't finish physically growing until around five years old, before maturing for another two years and reaching their prime between eight and 16 years old. Although they might slow down after this point, they are still extremely efficient; as Andy pointed out, a 60-year-old bricklayer might move slower than a young apprentice, but his experience makes him just as efficient. Ollie's huge heavy horse feet were captivating as we walked, clomping over the earth in slow, steady paces, with hooves so big I could probably wear one as an eccentric headpiece. Andy told me that he was trained in the basics of looking after horses' feet, but only farriers were qualified to shoe them. Ollie, however, was unshod, and when I asked why, Andy explained that one of the other horses had accidentally trodden on another one's foot and pulled his shoe off. Although the Percheron breed in general are known for the quality of their hooves, Andy joked that he had somehow found himself working with the only three Percherons in the world with terrible hooves, so after a successful trial season without shoes the previous year, they were now permanently unshod. I loved watching Ollie's huge feet press into the soil, soft and feathered, yet so strong and dangerous. An animal willing to submit to man, despite being able to crush him in a moment, if he wanted. Such is this beautiful and strange relationship we have built and nurtured over the centuries.

We arrived at the bakehouse, a stunning brick building with iron wall anchors, chimney pots and green painted windows. The information board told me it had originally been built in the seventeenth century in a village in Surrey before housing an extensive Victorian bakery; it was dismantled in the 1980s and rebuilt here. The clouds had now disappeared completely, and not even the cold spring wind was able to beat away the warmth of the sun as it filtered down to where Ollie stood, peaceful as ever, while the team unloaded his cart full of firewood for the baker's oven. One of the other visitors noticed his mane had been cropped short and Andy explained this was a process known as hogging, or 'roaching' in the United States. Hogging is the practice of shaving or cutting short a horse's mane, and in the case of heavy horses, often their leg feathers, too. It is an optional treatment, sometimes carried out to alter the horses' appearance, but more often to avoid infections and parasites. Andy explained that he hogged Ollie's mane because he often suffered with itching. A horse's mane, he went on to explain, is actually thought to have evolved to keep the horse's neck warm, by guiding rainwater off the body instead of it soaking into the skin. As horses' necks are much narrower than their bodies, this is also where heat loss can be the most severe, but as heavy horses are so bulky in their necks, too, it didn't make much difference to Ollie whether he had a mane or not. The tail, on the other hand, was important for keeping biting insects at bay, as anyone will know who has watched a fidgety horse in a field on a hot summer's day. And although their natural behaviour is to live in large herds, most horses will form only one or two close friendships within these groups. These two friends will then stand head to tail and nibble each other wherever they have an itch or an insect, gaining each other's trust in a position where they could easily be kicked in the head. It is through grooming our horses that we have managed to recreate a similar relationship, convincing them we are one of their herd mates instead of a non-equine threat.

As the team unloaded the cart, Ollie stood in the sun and nibbled his bit in an absent-minded way, suggesting to me that he was pretty happy with his role at this beautiful museum in the Sussex countryside. In fact, the only one who looked more content was Andy, leading him over the grass and patting him as he stopped by the bakehouse with a 'Good boy!' The early spring sunlight danced across the surface of the mill pond, where ducks and moorhens floated by as though completely oblivious that they were living in the twenty-first century rather than the seventeenth. The pace of life here was so slow and quiet, interrupted only by the murmur of visitors' voices as they sipped coffee and admired the architecture. And beneath it all was the scrape of Ollie's cart across the stone path, and the plod, plod, plod of his great heavy hooves, the epitome of power and grace encapsulated in four feathery feet.

CHAPTER NINE

Moorstone

My husband, daughter and I arrived under the cover of night fog after the inevitable delays of the A303 and then the winding roads of Dartmoor, hemmed in by a labyrinth of old, green lanes. Driving through the moor at night is particularly spooky because you are constantly on the alert for ponies, sheep and cattle, which enjoy sitting in the middle of the road, suddenly looming out of the darkness like white-eyed ghouls. When we approached the top of the hill near where we would be staying, the fog was polluted by a pale glow, as the floodlights of HMP Dartmoor broke out of their fortress reaching into the black sky. Escapes from UK prisons were fairly rare, but not even the high granite walls of Dartmoor were completely inescapable. Of the handful of notorious criminals who had broken out in the last century, Frank 'the Mad Axeman' Mitchell was perhaps the most famous, incarcerated after holding an elderly couple hostage with an axe. Allegedly with the help of Ronnie and Reggie Kray, Mitchell escaped in December 1966 while repairing fencing on Bagga Tor, telling the supervising prison officer he was off to 'feed some Dartmoor ponies'. Despite sparking the country's most extensive search for a prisoner, with 200 police officers, 100 Royal Marines and a Royal Air Force helicopter in tow, Mitchell was never seen again. His escape might have been successful, but he was likely killed as part of a gangland feud, possibly on the orders of the Krays. Dartmoor was one of my favourite places in the world, but on a dark and stormy night like this, struck by the sight of the grizzly prison and thoughts of axemen on the loose, it was a relief to finally reach our accommodation, an old coaching house behind a graveyard (because why not keep it spooky?). We locked the doors, lit the fire and devoured hot cross buns before putting Olive to bed and settling down to mark out our planned excursion for the following morning.

Back on the road the next day, the moor in daylight was a different place altogether. Still with its bleak, windswept tors and rocky outcrops, but beautiful in the morning light, shining in that magical way only Dartmoor can. But it was also raining in a way it can only rain in Dartmoor. Rivulets of water tumbled down the roads, rivers flowed where they shouldn't, fords rushed, and sponge-soaked moss glittered on every granite wall. The grey sky hung heavy over a barren moor, speckled with sheep and stones. In a few weeks, spring would set in, and the landscape would be rich with the hues of gorse blossom, bluebells and acid green birch leaves. But for now, there was a quiet beauty in the earth, the calm before the storm of spring. Migratory birds were still en route, the dawn chorus hadn't yet kicked off, and except for the snowdrops, there was only green and brown underfoot – the seeds and bulbs of future flowers were still waiting to detonate.

In the waterlogged moors that blanketed each tor, every now and then we found a trail of hoof marks – not cattle or sheep, but pony hooves; those of the Dartmoor ponies that had roamed this place for at least 3,500 years, and whose adaptation to the landscape had made them hardy and rugged, able to thrive on the poorest vegetation and harshest weather that shaped this part of England. Their calm temperament, strength and surefootedness were renowned, and it was because of their adaptability that they had historically been used for a range of industrial jobs and tasks, including mining, quarrying, shepherding, taking goods to market, and even helping the postman deliver the mail. There were several different types other than the pedigree Dartmoor pony, all ranging in colour between shades of brown, black and grey. In the sixteenth century, King Henry VIII decided that Dartmoor ponies, along with every other feral native breed around the country, were nothing more than 'little horses and nags of small stature', and ordered that any horses grazed on common land should be culled if they didn't measure a certain height; the story goes that he disliked any horse or pony that was too small to carry a knight. Fortunately, the rules were relaxed after his reign by his daughter Queen Elizabeth I, although it was thought that in remote, rural areas like Devon, Cornwall and Wales, nobody had been paying much attention to the rules anyway.

It is illegal to feed the ponies on Dartmoor and unwise to get too close. They are not handled like normal horses, and most spend a lot of their time roaming far from human hands. That doesn't mean, however, that there aren't a few opportunists ready to mob tourists when they get the chance. We pulled over into a passing place to check a location on my phone and noticed a few ponies standing at the edge of the road, rain-swept, and sparkly-eyed, and seemingly unbothered by our presence. In the short time it took to stop the car, google something and glance back up again, we found ourselves surrounded. A Dartmoor pony was standing beside each of our four car windows, eyes bright, ears pricked in search of something interesting – most likely food. This gang of yobs was clearly used to tourists pulling over here and offering treats of some kind, and although we didn't give them anything to eat, we couldn't help winding down the windows and offering a tickle instead. Soon enough, our car was full of horses' mouths dripping rain onto our laps, Olive cackling maniacally as a pony nuzzled her head in search of toddler crumbs. We knew they were 'wild' and we shouldn't be encouraging them, but there was something magical about having a moment of contact with an animal that belonged only to Dartmoor's wet heather flowers and wind-beaten tors. One of them pushed its nose so close to my face that I surrendered and gave it a little kiss. So close up, I could see fronds of moss stuck to its coat, fresh mud and rainwater and the whole of Dartmoor in fragments across its neck. And best of all, that universal aroma that all horses have, no matter how wild or tame. The infinitely comforting scent of sunlight, grass, earth, dust, sweat, rain and hay that's found only in the warmth of a horse's coat.

When we talk about Dartmoor ponies, the name is really an umbrella term for two different types. The first is the pedigree Dartmoor pony, recognised as a rare breed by the Rare Breeds Survival Trust, and typical of the ponies seen in the showring at country shows. The origins of the pedigree Dartmoor date back to 1869, when polo was first introduced to the UK and the quest to breed suitable polo ponies began. Valued for their sure-footedness and speed, Dartmoors were crossbred with thoroughbreds, Arabs and hackneys, and by 1899 a local committee had been set up to oversee the registration of Dartmoor ponies, creating the official breed. Crossbreeding with Arabs was encouraged in breeding circles, to the point where they had to place restrictions on how much of the horse was a different breed to ensure there was enough of the native Dartmoor still in the bloodline. Today, ponies must meet certain criteria to qualify as a pedigree Dartmoor by proving they are from official breeding stock and displaying a number of physical characteristics, such as the correct height, colouring, shape and movement as specified by the Dartmoor Pony Society.

The second type, known more generally as the Dartmoor hill pony, refers to those animals without a registered purebred bloodline; these are considered by many to be the closest Dartmoor has to indigenous ponies, and range widely in height, size, colouring and build. When we hear old stories and myths about the ponies of Dartmoor, it is usually these to which they refer. On dark and stormy nights, for example, it was rumoured that smugglers used the hill ponies to carry their contraband, selectively breeding the darkest animals to avoid being spotted in the moonlight. It would have been the hill ponies, too, that were used for mining, quarrying and all other heavy labour, as purebred animals would have been too highly prized to be designated such strenuous work.

We left the ponies to their attempted looting, and drove on through the moor. As lovely as they were, we hadn't actually come to visit the ponies, although we assumed they would make an appearance at some point. Instead, we were here to unearth a bit of industrial archaeology. We had come to visit the site of an abandoned granite quarry, one of the many scars of industry pockmarked across the British landscape, particularly in Devon, Cornwall and Wales. The influence of mining and quarrying was still an important part of the cultural heritage here in the south-west, so much so that several locations in Cornwall and West Devon had been designated as UNESCO World Heritage Sites. During the eighteenth and nineteenth centuries, these landscapes were transformed as a result of the rapid growth of pioneering copper and tin mining; this growth brought along innovative new infrastructure that enabled mines to be carved deeper underground than ever before, along with new engine houses, foundries, towns, smallholdings, canals, tramroads, railways, ports and harbours up on the surface. Because of this surge, the region was at one point producing two-thirds of the world's supply of copper, and the technology that was developed here went on to have a huge influence on international mining practices through the nineteenth century and beyond.

As with most of the industries that have shaped the British Isles over the years, horses played an integral role in mining and quarrying around the UK. The mining horse, or 'pit pony' as it became known, was first used to transport coal from the collieries to the customer, as well as winding and pumping the engines. It wasn't until later they were moved underground, transporting coal from the coalface to the shaft, ready to be hauled above ground. One of the reasons for this was the need to replace women and children, whose work in the mines was seen by many as inhumane. Young children were required to crawl on their hands and knees, pulling carts of coal behind them, for hours at a time, often never seeing daylight. Women, too, spent most of their daylight hours in the mines, many of whom were pregnant and ended up giving birth below ground. It wasn't until an accident in 1838 at the Huskar Colliery in Silkstone, Yorkshire, when 26 children drowned, that the general public found out who really worked in the mines; a media-driven outcry followed, and in 1842 a report was published detailing the full extent of working life in the mines. Despite objections from colliery owners, over the next few years the industry brought in regulations to improve conditions, although it would take many more decades for children to be banned from the mines completely.

As women and children were encouraged to find work elsewhere, the role of mining horses expanded, and many were moved underground. By 1878, the Royal Society for the Prevention of Cruelty to Animals (RSPCA) estimated there were over 200,000 horses at work in British mines, and despite their 'pit pony' status, most were actually large horses whose strength was required for heavy haulage. Some of the best-looking enjoyed a more privileged life as they were taken above ground to compete in exhibitions, and only given light duties to keep them healthy and handsome. But for most, they endured the same conditions and dangers as the miners themselves, with hundreds dying from mistreatment, accidents and explosions, and plenty never seeing sunlight again once they disappeared into the darkness. In shaft mines, it was difficult and time-consuming to move the ponies underground; some early drawings show them being tied to a lift with leather straps and then lowered down, while others were sent in one-by-one using a cage lift. Time meant money, so to save both, the ponies were usually stabled underground. Those animals working in drift and slope mines, which had horizontal entrances instead of vertical ones, were luckier. Their stables were close to the mine entrance so they could at least see sunlight and feel the fresh air; they were also brought above ground more regularly, and could walk in and out rather than 'taking' the lift.

The difference between a tolerable and intolerable life was often down to the men who handled them; while there were plenty who treated the animals poorly, most formed a strong bond with their horses and ensured their working conditions were as comfortable as possible, bringing them extra food, caring for their tack and equipment, and treating them like the sentient creatures they were. Many even trusted their horses with their own safety, believing them to have a 'sixth sense' that could alert them to danger, and following their behavioural cues as a result. In 1904, one young miner named John William Bell, who worked in the Elsecar Colliery near Barnsley, was awarded a medal for kindness by the Association for the Prevention of Cruelty to Pit Ponies, after saving his pony's life when a group of miners became trapped underground. While most of the human workers escaped through a small opening, he decided to stay with his pony to give it a better chance of rescue, as he knew a human life was seen to be more worthy of saving. His gamble paid off and they were both rescued, and his story was used to promote better treatment of mining ponies. In 1911, a study by the Royal Commission exposed the terrible conditions in which most pit ponies lived, including the fact that the average lifespan was only three and a half years, compared with 20 or more years above ground. And in 1911, the British Coal Mines Act led to tougher laws to protect the ponies, including a minimum working pony age of four years, as well as obligatory vet checks and shodding them with proper horseshoes.

Most of the old mines and quarries in the south-west are now closed or abandoned, although the landscape still holds clues to their existence in its place names, buildings, streets, valleys and tors. There are, however, some old sites still open to the public, by way of the overground remnants, underground sites turned to museums, or spaces like abandoned open-pit quarries that are, by their nature, less dangerous to explore than pitch-black shafts dropping thousands of feet into the ground. Once depleted of their resources, quarries are usually closed, and unless they are turned into a golf course or race track, they are often reclaimed by nature. Providing any pollutants are removed, these scars scratched out of the landscape do not take long to heal, being open to the sky and full of bare patches of ground waiting to be recolonised by plants. Many are handed over to local authorities or conservation groups who manage the sites as nature reserves; examples of these include the Buriton chalk pits near my home in Hampshire, Bole Hill in the Peak District, and Salthill Quarry in Clitheroe.

It was one of these abandoned quarries that had drawn us to Dartmoor that weekend. After asking for directions in the visitor centre, we parked the car and crossed the road that wove around the edge of Haytor Down, a rocky granite outcrop that was formed over 280 million years ago. We began our gentle ascent up the boggy slope of the tor, waterlogged with a carpet of sphagnum moss that had soaked up every drop of rain it could. This moss played a crucial role in the creation of Europe's peat bogs, able to hold water in their spongy bodies long after the surrounding soil dries out. In holding on to the water, they keep essential nutrients in place and help prevent the decay of dead plant material, and it is this material that will eventually be compressed over hundreds of years to finally form the rare and precious substance we call peat. Aside from providing a home to thousands of species of wildlife, including butterflies, dragonflies, snipe, curlew, merlins, skylarks, and plants like bog asphodel, marsh violet, sundews and marsh willowherb, peat also stores vast amounts of carbon; in fact, estimates show that it is so important that peat be kept in the ground, that just a five per cent loss would equal as much as the UK's annual greenhouse gas emissions. They also help reduce flood risk and filter the water, which I could see before my eyes. As my feet stepped into the soft earth, small pools of water appeared, so astonishingly clear that I could see every detail of the moss spores lying underneath. This bright, wet little world in miniature was the stuff of folklore; a place for sprites and pixies. Unfortunately, commercial peat extraction was removing 500 years' worth of growth every year, using it for, among other things, compost, heating and bedding for horses' stables. Luckily, this protected stretch of sphagnum moss looked far from decimated, and once we had left the boggy base of the tor and climbed higher up the slope, the ground shifted from bog to stone, with firmer, more boot-friendly paths winding gently through the rocks. Not only were these paths easier to walk on but they were perfectly designed to traverse the tricky surface of the tor, whose ridges were speckled with sharp boulders and tufts of thick grass. A few steps further up onto the summit of the tor and we found what we were looking for.

Humans have lived and worked on Haytor Down for thousands of years, but it wasn't until the nineteenth century that it became one of the industrial hubs of Dartmoor. The reason for this was hidden in the dramatic, craggy landscape that had been slowly unfolding for around 300 million years, and whose foundations were laid in the geological period

known as the Carboniferous. At this time, the landmass that
we call Britain could be found somewhere around the
Equator, while Dartmoor was completely submerged
beneath the sea. Over millions of years, large swathes of
muddy sediment accumulated at the bottom of this sea and
eventually turned into rock. Later, major movements in the
Earth's surface caused parts of 'Britain' to buckle and fold,
thrusting the deep sea sediments above water and shaping
them into mountains. A mass of molten rock was then
injected deep into the heart of the mountain range, which
cooled over millions of years to form what we now call
granite, a rock made of three types of coarse mineral crystals:
quartz, feldspar and mica. The liquid rock also contained
smaller deposits of rare metals, such as tin, copper, lead and
iron, which formed in the cracks and fissures as the granite
cooled. In the hundreds of millions of years since the
mountains emerged, they have been slowly worn away by
the wind, rain and frost, so that today, the top of the granite
layer is exposed to the open sky, and forms a visible upland
'spine', stretching from the Isles of Scilly through West
Penwith, Carnmenellis, St Austell, Bodmin Moor and, at the
easternmost point, Dartmoor. It is here, in the National
Park, that the largest outcrop of granite can be found,
embedded within a layer of older sedimentary rocks. After a
spell of tin and copper extraction from the medieval period
onwards, metal mining operations on Haytor came to an
end in the nineteenth century, by which time the abundance
of granite in the area had already drawn its own form of
commercial attention.

Prized for its toughness and resilience, granite has been
used in the construction of homes, buildings and walls on
Dartmoor for thousands of years. But it wasn't until three
centuries ago that demand grew from small-scale, local
extraction, removing surface-level blocks known as
'moorstone', to a full-scale commercial enterprise that dug
deep into the earth and exported Haytor granite around

the world. This change was catalysed by the opening of the granite tramway in 1820, a line of carefully placed stones that ran from the quarry at Haytor Down to the canal at Ventiford, 8.5 miles away; from here, the goods could be loaded onto barges and carried to the Teign estuary for export, mostly to London – Haytor granite was used in the construction of London Bridge, the British Museum and many other notable structures and monuments. When it was first built, the tramway was made of end-to-end blocks of granite almost 2m long, along which the wheels of the wagons could roll, pulled by the quarry ponies and their handlers. Each wagon could carry up to 3 tonnes of granite, and shipping it down from the tor required no power at all as they could simply roll down the hill with a braking pole pushed against the rim of the wheel, powered by the magic of gravity; ponies were then employed in teams of 12 to pull the loaded wagons up from the quarry site at Holwell Tor, before bringing the empty wagons back from the canal.

Although the main tracks of the tramway had been carted off long ago, the base level of stone remained – and it was this that we came upon as we climbed to the summit of Haytor Rock. Old and weathered by horses' hooves, cartwheels, and decades of Dartmoor wind and rain, the tramway seemed to be almost sinking back into the earth, back to the darkness in which it was formed, so slowly, by the creeping passage of time. There were lichens scraped over the surface of the stones, mint-green and milk-white, and notched carvings that looked like ancient runes, but that we later discovered were just marks from the feather-and-tare method of cutting stone. From our view at the top of the slope, we could see the tramway winding down to the east through moss and boulder, over the tor and down into the far distance. And to the west, it disappeared behind another huge mass of rock coated in greenery. Dave had already wandered off that way with Olive, so I followed the path up through an ocean of oozing mosses, stopping now and then to stare into the pools left behind by the tiny hoofprints of Dartmoor ponies, imprinted microcosms full of spores and insects that would thrive until the sun returned and the pools disappeared once more, springing back to sweet sphagnum cushions. When the wind dropped, all I could hear across the tor was the sound of trickling water – falling through the air, pouring through the moss at my feet, pulsing and sighing through the entire hill. I tracked the hoofprints up the slope to where Dave and Olive stood waiting, beckoning for me and the dogs to follow so they could show us what they had discovered, hidden among the rocks.

The rain had poured all morning and kept most people inside, which meant we had the remains of Haytor Quarry all to ourselves. A lagoon enclosed by turrets of stone as tall as the sky; sanctuary from the wind, and only the *drip drip drip* of the rain that tumbled from the trees into a pool as clear as cut glass. In the centre, a rusted old winch, the colour of milk chocolate, lay half-submerged in the water. If it weren't for the slightly wonky angle, and the fact that there was nobody here except us, it could have still been in perfect use; Dave even had a go on the handle, and it worked, albeit redundant without the derrick that would have once been attached, a kind of long, wooden crane that was operated by hand, pivoting to haul stones onto the tramway carts. At some point it had fallen or been dismantled and now lay next to the winch, rotting in the water like a ship's mast. These industrial artefacts were the only clues that this peaceful lagoon had once been a profitable quarry. Here and there, we spotted more of the feather-and-tare notches around the edge of the pool, secret codes from the past whispering a way of life known only to those who had since returned to the earth. Those who pulled and strained and mined the quarry for precious stone, carting it away and out into the world by way of their weather-worn horses. Decades later, there was very little movement left in its wake; only our dogs dipping their noses into the water, and swaying trees at the quarry edge, and a bloom of pink flowers that clung to the rocks higher up, dancing in the Dartmoor wind. This felt like a safe, secret space; once gutted and abandoned by humans, and now passing back, stone by glistening stone, into the healing bosom of the earth.

♘

Quarries like Haytor were entirely dependent on both human labour and horsepower, and although it would have been difficult, heavy work for the horses, particularly on warm days when the wind dropped and the sun hammered down onto this unsheltered landscape, it must have been a better life than those of the horses that worked underground. The intensity of commercial quarrying exposed the inner workings of the Earth to the sky, but with that came clean air and sunshine, pouring into the wounds of industry that had been torn across the moor. Hundreds of feet below, the same Earth was plundered, but for the animals that worked down there, clean air and sunshine were luxuries that many went weeks, months or even years without.

The narrative woven by a piece of Haytor granite was a relatively simple one – cut, hauled and rolled along on the tramway, ready to meet the sculptor who would give it a new life as a statue, a bridge or an art gallery. But for the owners of the subterranean mines who sought deeper deposits of tin, copper, iron, silver-lead and arsenic, their path to success was a little more convoluted – and horses were vital to every step. The reason for this was the material itself; metal deposits are locked away inside naturally occurring rock called ore, which means that mining the ore is only the first step in the long process of unearthing, refining, valuing and selling metal. Imagine a lump of ore being found in one of the many shafts that were once carved out beneath the Tamar Valley mining district on the south-west edge of Dartmoor, a beautiful stretch of exposed moorland, farmland and deep wooded dells that straddles the border of Cornwall and Devon. The lump could have been tin ore, also known as cassiterite. Once mined and carted to the shaft by the horses underground, it might have been hauled up using a horse gin (a word thought to derive from 'engine'), in which up to four horses were harnessed to a wheel, walking in a circle to engage the gears, turn the drum and raise the baskets of minerals from the mineshaft. Above ground, pack horses and carts were used to transport the ore to blowing houses, which contained a furnace and a pair of bellows, powered by an adjacent water wheel. Once processed and cast into blocks, the tin was packed onto another horse-drawn cart and taken to be processed for coinage, a taxing system on refined tin that was so influential to the local economy, entire 'stannary' towns sprouted up wherever lucrative mines tunnelled down.

Smoke drifting from smelting chimneys; the clink of miners' carts rolling through the dark; horses' hooves echoing up narrow shafts; the creaking of the stamp mill pounding rocks to rubble; it is difficult to imagine so much industrial movement sweeping over the Dartmoor landscape, whose bleak, beautiful tors are now so still, the silence broken only by snipe and curlew lurking in the heather blossom. The remnants of 40 blowing houses can still be seen on Dartmoor today and there is at least one place on the moor that has not only lifted the story of Dartmoor's mines out of the history books – it has brought an entire mine back to life.

Technically, the Kelly Mine was never completely dead – it only closed in 1951, and the site was abandoned where it stood on the eastern edge of the National Park. The company running the operation owed the landowner for rent and royalties on the ore they had been extracting, a deposit of micaceous iron oxide known locally as 'shiny ore', used for ink blotting, pottery glazing and its most common use today, to make anti-corrosion paint. In lieu of payment of their debts, the mining company left all their machinery behind, which stayed there for more than 30 years before the landowner agreed to lease the whole site to a group of mining enthusiasts. The Kelly Mine Preservation Society's team of volunteers have been restoring and preserving it ever since, refurbishing the machinery and processing plant so thoroughly that they are now in full working order.

We visited the Kelly Mine on our way home from Dartmoor, after a kind staff member in Dartmoor's visitor centre told us about it. We were intrigued by her description – there were no signs for the site, but if we aimed roughly for a certain point on a certain road, we would see cars parked along the edge of a quiet stretch of woodland. We reached the place and walked along the wall until we came to a small gate; on stepping through, we were immediately greeted by one of the volunteers. We had found the mine! To anyone stumbling upon it without a wider context, it might have seemed like a shabby old yard, full of scrap metal, train tracks and pieces of broken machinery. But as soon as our volunteer guide started showing us round, we knew we had struck gold (or shiny ore). We spent the next hour touring the site, Olive more interested in the sticks and pine cones than the mining operation that ran here less than a century ago. Peering into the dark void of the adit (mine entrance), we then visited the shaft itself, followed by a demonstration of the washing, jigging and stamping of the ore, a trip to the settling tanks, waterwheel and tramway, and then into the drying shed where the final product – a kind of grey, shimmering dust – was weighed and dispatched in huge, wooden barrels. We had never in our lives thought ourselves mine enthusiasts, but it was honestly one of the most enjoyable hours we had ever spent. And as with every mining and quarrying industry of its time, even here in this quiet woodland glade, the marks left by horses were clear to see. Not only were the horses responsible for carting the shiny ore away to be sold, but the sign on a small cart sledge displayed in the drying room told us there were more workings further up on the Kelly Mine site, with evidence of sledge tracks leading down to the processing site. Our guide told us the mine would have had its own small pony, most likely a native Dartmoor, responsible for hauling the cart up and down through the trees, a steep path that only a small and stocky pony could tackle with ease.

The Kelly Mine might have lasted a few decades into the twentieth century, but most of the mines and quarries in south-west England had declined or disappeared by the 1900s, if not long before. Haytor Quarry was struggling as early as 1834, when the workers were recorded as being unpaid and in an 'unsettled state', suggesting the industry was in trouble. This slump continued until 1841, when parish accounts record most of the local dwellings as empty as the workforce dispersed. By the 1860s, most of the local quarries had been abandoned and the tramway had fallen into disuse. Extraction trudged on until the 1880s and the last recorded granite was quarried from Haytor for use in the Exeter War Memorial after the First World War. Many more mines and quarries closed in the 1890s, causing a diaspora of Cornish and Devonian people who left England to seek their fortunes elsewhere. In each decade from 1861 to 1901, around a fifth of the area's male population migrated abroad, mostly made up of miners, farmers, merchants and tradesmen. Of those with mining experience, tens of thousands were inspired to try their luck in the Californian and Australian gold fields, with profits being sent home to their families to try and keep them out of the workhouse. As a result of these industries winding down, hundreds of horses were gradually retired from their work and returned to the farms, fields and factories above ground.

Having toiled underground in some capacity since the 1700s, it was the end of an era for working horses as their numbers slowly declined throughout the twentieth century, after a peak of 70,000 in 1913. By the time the National Coal Board was set up in 1947, there were only 21,000 working horses, and by 1984, their numbers had fallen to just 55. Although industry changes were the main driving force behind the decline of working horses, it also reflected a societal shift in the way animals were being treated. The nineteenth and twentieth centuries saw the creation of the RSPCA in 1824, followed by the Royal Society for the Protection of Birds (RSPB) in 1889 and the Wildlife Trusts in 1912, marking the beginning of a gradual change in our relationship with animals, especially working animals that had, until now, been seen more as machines than sentient beings. As Anna Sewell wrote in her best-selling 1877 novel *Black Beauty*:

> There is no religion without love, and people may talk as much as they like about their religion, but if it does not teach them to be good and kind to man and beast, it is all a sham.

Sewell's 'autobiographical' tale, told through the eyes of one of England's working horses, reflected the wider shift in attitudes toward animal welfare and in 1886, it inspired a London woman named Ann Lindo to found the Home of Rest for Horses (now known as the Horse Trust), to create a sanctuary for London's working cab horses. These animals worked long, hard shifts with little rest – not because their owners didn't care for them, but because they depended too heavily on the money their horses brought in for them each day. Lindo created a sanctuary for sick and exhausted horses to rest, while other, healthier animals were sent out in their place. The owners could still earn a living and after a few months of recovery, the original horse could be returned to them, refreshed and ready to work. The project was hugely successful and drew plenty of support, including from Prince Albert; today, it is still backed by royalty, with Princess Anne, a lifelong lover of horses, being the charity's current patron. The Horse Trust now has four main focus areas: providing lifetime sanctuary for retired equines; promoting horse welfare; funding research into horse health, and educating people about horse welfare and ownership. It still provides a safe, comfortable sanctuary for around 140 retired horses, ponies and donkeys in their 'Home of Rest' in Buckinghamshire.

It wasn't until 1999 that the last two working pit ponies in Britain retired, from the Pant y Gaseg mine near Pontypool; and the practice of stabling ponies underground only came to an end in 1994, when a pony called Flax was brought to the surface for the final time, having worked at the Ellington Colliery in Northumberland. In Wales, pit ponies played such an important role in the cultural, economic and natural heritage of the entire country that they were commemorated in a huge earthwork sculpture designed by Mike Petts in the 1990s. Built using thousands of tons of coal shale waste material left behind when the Penallta Colliery closed, the sculpture takes the shape of a galloping horse, roaming free across the sweet, green meadows of the Rhymney Valley. At 200m from hoof to muzzle, the sculpture is a living monument to an industry that drove Britain through the Industrial Revolution and placed Wales and its people at the heart of global shipping and trade. Not only does it celebrate the lives of the horses who worked above and below the Welsh landscape, but visitors can follow a walking trail along the sculpture's spine, surrounded by a carpet of cowslips in spring.

Giant hoofprints have also been scattered through the surrounding fields, which fill with water in heavy rain and create more habitats for wildlife. Originally anonymous, the locals decided to name the sculpture Sultan, after one of the last pit ponies to have worked in the mine before it closed its doors forever.

CHAPTER TEN

War

In the centre of my town there is a market square that, for hundreds of years, has been a thoroughfare for traders and townspeople. Rooted in the trade of sheep, horses, cattle and the produce of local cottage industries, it is still a thriving market place today – although the livestock has now been replaced by fresh fruit and sourdough loaves. The twice-weekly market days were also the best place to find, in my opinion, the best chocolate brownie in town, and I sat on the edge of the square to eat one, gazing up at a statue that stood in the middle of the square. It had been standing there for so long, and I had looked at it so many times, I ought to have known every inch of it by now. Olive was also admiring it between sticky mouthfuls of brownie, because it was a 'horsey!' – and she really loves horseys.

The horsey in question was standing on a plinth with one foreleg raised and his head held high. Sitting on his back was a man in Roman costume, a sword sheathed on one side and in the opposite hand, a scroll. His name was William III, otherwise known as William of Orange, a Dutch-born English king, remembered for defeating the Catholic James II in the Battle of the Boyne in 1690, and becoming a figurehead for Protestant 'salvation'. The statue had always seemed an impressive one considering its location in the market square of a sleepy Hampshire town. Commissioned in 1750 by a local MP, it first stood in front of a mansion house before its demolition caused the statue to be relocated here. The crumbling inscription on the plinth commemorates King William's services to the nation, and there are still marks here and there from when the statue was once gilded with colour. But the overall impression is one of power and victory, two themes that are common among equestrian statues like these, celebrating those who fought for a cause they believed in – and the animals that carried them into battle.

There are more than 80 equestrian statues around the UK, many themed around warfare, battles and victories of one kind or another. A popular urban myth claims that you can work out the manner of someone's death by the position of the horse in their statue: one hoof lifted means the rider sustained serious injuries in battle and possibly died later; two hooves lifted means they died in battle, and all four hooves on the ground mean they were never injured in battle and died by other means. This rule is not consistently followed, but people still use it nonetheless to try and decode the stories behind the stones. The statue in Petersfield bears the inscription *William III* on its plinth, but when you look at the piece in its entirety, there is far more horse than man on display. It demonstrates how most of our best-remembered historical events relied on horsepower to carry out the desires of men, particularly on the battlefield, yet so rarely shared in their glory. And although this horse seemed calmer and more peaceful than a typical warhorse, it still brought the concept of conflict into the heart of this quiet, cheerful town – one whose surrounding fields were full of horses that, not so long ago, would have been taken by law and sent away, over the glittering sea, to fall in battle at the hands of man.

Horses have been used in war for centuries, but it wasn't until the medieval period that they were first intensively bred for such a purpose. Around the eighth or ninth century, Europeans came into close contact with Arabian horses for the first time due to the Islamic conquest of Spain and the English crusades in Asia. Records show a deliberate rise in Arabian stock from this point onwards, suggesting they were highly valued – most likely for their speed, endurance and adaptability that came from surviving in scorching desert landscapes. For the first time, proper breeding studs were set up in England, often to produce warhorses with optimal characteristics for the battlefield, and by the late medieval period, the modern breeds we still see today had started to emerge. Aside from the popular destriers, coursers and rounceys of the medieval period, breeders experimented to create new ways to weaponize their horses. The Teutonic Knights, an order of monks founded to protect crusading Christians in the Holy Lands, fought with geldings from high-quality stock which became known as 'monk horses'. As they were castrated, the advantage was that if their horses were captured by the enemy, they could not be used to improve local bloodstock and the crusaders' horses would remain superior. This kind of intensive breeding, however, brought weaknesses as well as strengths; like with all pedigree and intensively managed animals, the reduction in genetic diversity began to cause health problems that are still persistent today.

U

In the year 350BC, an Athenian historian, philosopher and soldier called Xenophon wrote a manual on the care and training of horses. Full of advice on breaking young colts, feeding, grooming, training and preparing for battle, *On Horsemanship* would later be considered one of the first books to educate its readers on compassionately fine-tuning the relationship between horse and rider:

> If one induces the horse to assume that carriage which it would adopt of its own accord when displaying its beauty, then one directs the horse to appear joyous and magnificent, proud and remarkable for having been ridden.

The book also helped to lay the foundations for what would not only become an Olympic sport over 2,000 years later but would also be considered one of the most challenging displays of competence a rider can perform. The skills required became known collectively as dressage, from the French word *dresseur*, meaning 'training'; it has also been called the 'ballet of equestrianism'. The rider must work with their horse to develop suppleness, flexibility, obedience and athleticism, which in turn help to create a more harmonious relationship between horse and rider. To demonstrate these skills, riders must perform a set of prescribed movements in front of a panel of judges; depending on the test level, this could include anything from gentle walking and trotting in straight lines and circles, to a cantering zigzag, pirouette, leg yield (where the horse travels forwards and sideways simultaneously), piaffe (a trot on the spot), passage (a powerful trot) or flying change where the horse changes the leading leg while in the air. When performed correctly and with the appropriate training, dressage is not cruel to horses; rather the idea is to strengthen the bond between horse and rider through precise, gentle methods for, as Xenophon himself pointed out, 'anything forced is not beautiful.'

Like my short-lived polo career, my own experience of dressage was limited but I did compete in an introductory test when I was at university. A few walks and trots; circles and straight lines; trying my best to look neat and tidy. It was yet another situation where someone suggested we try something new and we all said 'yes' without much thought – but it did end up being incredibly fun and much less frightening than polo! Being a student, I shared a six-bedroom house with eight other people, so between weekly lessons I marked out the arena letters on my bedroom floor and trotted around my room in tiny circles, trying my best to remember each part of the test. Joyously, my efforts paid off; I passed the test and came sixth, which meant I went home with my first ever shiny purple rosette. Sadly, my time at university came to an end shortly afterwards, and I stopped riding with the club, but I would love to take another test one day, if only to bring home some more ribbons.

Of the three equestrian disciplines performed at the Olympic Games – dressage, eventing and show jumping – dressage might not have the speed and adrenaline of its counterparts, but it requires just as much skill and strength. In fact, the art of dressage as we know it today was actually developed as a military training technique in the sixteenth and seventeenth centuries, with the sporting side arriving much later in the 1800s. When dressage was made an Olympic sport in the 1912 Games in Stockholm, it was performed exclusively by male military officers, and it wasn't until 1952 in Helsinki that the competition was opened up to civilians – and to women. One of the first female competitors was Lis Hartel from Denmark, who had contracted polio at 23 years old and remained permanently paralysed below the knee. Despite having further issues with her arms and hands, and being unable to mount or dismount unassisted, she went on to win the silver medal – the first to be won by any woman in any individual sport when in direct competition with men at the Olympics.

The strong values of dressage – producing obedient, supple and responsive horses – were perfectly suited to the military training grounds of Renaissance Europe. The better schooled your horse, the better they would perform in battle, and it didn't hurt that a high-ranking soldier could be observed in public, mounted on a beautiful horse that moved in such a way that nobody could question their ability as a horseman. One of the early advocates of dressage in Britain was William Cavendish, 1st Duke of Newcastle and a renowned horse breeder. Sharing Xenophon's more compassionate, sympathetic way of training horses, in 1658 he wrote the hugely influential book *A General System of Horsemanship*, which had a lasting and far-reaching influence on the art of riding all over the world. From this point onwards, the military training of horses moved away from the brutality of the mounted knight and embraced the concept of the cavalry horse – ranging in size, weight and speed depending on the task required of them, but all trained to their different strengths, and valued for their brains as much as their build. Large, heavy horses were used to break enemy formations; small, light horses and their riders were used to scout new areas and chase down targets, as well as becoming specialist marksmen who could shoot accurately from long distances; fast horses carried important orders and news between commanders and their officers, and provided their riders with a quick getaway in case of defeat; and tall horses gave their riders a clear view across the battlefield, although this also made them prime targets for enemy shooters.

Around one-third of the horses historically used by the British Army were trained as mounts for soldiers. Their roles were varied and the animals were intelligent and disciplined, which meant the British cavalry often dominated the battlefields in which they fought. But that wasn't always the case. In 1854, war broke out between the Russian Empire and an alliance of British, French, Sardinian and Ottoman troops. The conflict – known as the Crimean War – centred on who would have influence in the declining Ottoman Empire; the major battleground was the Crimea, a peninsula in eastern Europe surrounded by the Black Sea and the Sea of Azov. In the autumn of that year, British and French soldiers landed in the Crimea with the objective of attacking Russia's naval base and weakening its presence in the Black Sea. By October, a battle had broken out near the city of Balaklava, but through a miscommunication of orders, a brigade of over 600 horsemen charged headlong into a valley ringed on three sides by Russian infantry and artillery, armed only with their sabres and lances. The soldiers were part of the British Light Cavalry, and were riding unarmoured, fast horses intended for cutting down enemy units as they tried to retreat. But the instructions relayed by their commanders were vague and misdirected, and they ended up riding the mile-and-a-quarter-long charge with

Russians shooting at them from every direction. With a 40 per cent human casualty rate and around 375 of the horses wounded, it is still considered one of Britain's most tragic and celebrated cavalry charges, and was immortalised in Alfred Tennyson's poem, 'The Charge of the Light Brigade', written just a few weeks afterwards to commemorate those who rode 'into the valley of Death':

> Cannon to right of them,
> Cannon to left of them,
> Cannon behind them
> Volleyed and thundered;
> Stormed at with shot and shell,
> While horse and hero fell.
> They that had fought so well
> Came through the jaws of Death,
> Back from the mouth of hell,
> All that was left of them,
> Left of six hundred.

Somehow, the Light Brigade managed to reach its destination, where the remaining soldiers crashed into the enemy lines with a vengeance, before staggering back along a causeway of broken bodies and artillery shells. The valley, according to one corporal, was engulfed in smoke and blood: 'the flame, the smoke, the roar were in our faces. It was like riding into the mouth of a volcano.'

U

The British Army has not used horses in a combat role since the First World War, when more than one million animals were sent abroad to the front line. It was here on the Western Front, a 400-mile-long stretch of land weaving through France and Belgium, that horses lived alongside men in the cold, sodden trenches, carrying troops and supplies, hauling heavy weaponry, and when the time came, leading the charge into battle. A quarter of a million horses fell on the Western Front alone, faced with adversaries they had never encountered in their lives back home. Instead of towns, fields and farms, they were surrounded by bullets, rifle fire, shell explosions, thick mud, blood-soaked bodies – and everywhere, always, the lingering scent of death.

Not only were they needed for physical conflict, but horses played an essential role in the huge infrastructure that existed behind the front line; almost anything too heavy to lift, from mail bags and rations, to equipment, ammunition and other supplies, was carried by horse-drawn cart. Some were even used to lay telephone cable, with a rider on horseback rolling out a cable drum as the horse galloped along in front. Throughout the course of the war, around 1,000 horses were shipped to Europe every single day. But they also had to be kept safe and well when they arrived, especially as many of the soldiers who would be handling them had never done so before. The Blue Cross had been founded in 1897 as 'Our Dumb Friends League' to care for working horses on the streets of London and, during the First World War, issued manuals to troops with basic instructions on horse anatomy, care and wellbeing. It developed a 'Blue Cross Fund' to care for horses on the battlefield and by 1918 had raised today's equivalent of £6.5million used to treat over 50,000 horses. The Blue Cross also provided tools such as hoof picks and nose bags, which were used to make sure the horses didn't waste any of their precious feed. The British Army believed in keeping its horses fatter so they could better cope with the bleak conditions of the trenches – and the theory paid off. While there was more horse feed shipped from the UK to the Western Front than ammunition, the British lost half as many horses as the French, who rationed their food more and kept them in a leaner condition. Vets were also on hand to help those horses who suffered illness or injury, with 80 per cent of those treated by the army veterinary corps recovering sufficiently enough to be sent straight back into service. For those who weren't so lucky, a tool called a farrier's axe was used to put a mortally wounded horse out of its misery, as well as chopping off the one hoof that had been stamped with the regiment's number. This way, they could account for the ones that had been killed, and guarantee these valuable animals hadn't been captured alive by the enemy.

Away from the battlefield, a small number of horses stayed on British soil while still playing an important role in the war. On the quayside outside the Museum of Liverpool, a monument to the Liverpool working horse, titled *Waiting*, was designed by sculptor Judy Boyt and unveiled in 2010. The bronze horse stands waiting for his next load on the docks, strong yet gentle, and with the cockle-shell-shaped blinkers around his eyes that were unique to the working horses of Liverpool. For more than 300 years, horses had been used to move goods between the docks and inner-city businesses, as there was no direct railway connection to most of the seven-mile-long quayside estate. Not only were commercial goods carried by horse-drawn cart for centuries, but during both world wars, they kept supply lines open and ensured the city's economy and communities could stay afloat.

Despite their contributions to life in wartime Britain, the reality was that horses became a much rarer sight on British soil as the conflict continued. When war first broke out in 1914, the British Army had only 25,000 horses at its disposal. Just as it needed more men to bolster the forces in France, it also needed more horses – and there was only one way to get both in a short amount of time. The Army Remount Department travelled around the country with conscription papers in hand, looking for horses that were fit for purpose, regardless of their occupation. Those used to drawing ploughs and pulling inner-city cabs became warhorses overnight, with 120,000 called into service in the first few weeks alone. Hundreds of thousands more were shipped in from North America, Canada and Australia, risking disease and enemy warships to join the Allies in Europe. And to accompany the horses, thousands more officers and men were conscripted or promoted to cope specifically with the increased stock of horses, particularly from groups like the landed gentry, masters of foxhounds and others who had experience on horseback. One of these was the Scottish-Australian poet Will H. Ogilvie, who was in charge of preparing the Canadian horses for military service, and wrote a number of poems inspired by his love of horses, hunting and peace after war. Today, his 1922 poem 'The Hoofs of the Horses' is still often read at the funerals of farriers.

Although the mass export of horses brought reinforcements to the battlefields, a huge void was inevitably opened in the farms, fields and cities they left behind. When the men were sent away to fight, the women of Britain were able to step up and take on new roles that had previously been exclusively occupied by men, including as farm workers, tractor drivers, train cleaners, bus conductors, volunteer police officers and transporting coal on canal barges. But as the horses began to disappear, options were limited when it came to replacing them. Those who relied on horsepower for their living tried to plead with the government to think more carefully before conscripting animals for war, including the writer and illustrator Beatrix Potter, who had opposed the government's proposal that farm horses be subject to conscription if conflict arose, several years before the First World War broke out. Having bought a number of working farms near her Hill Top home in the Lake District, Potter relied on horsepower for ploughing, and felt so passionately about the cause that it led her to become involved in national politics for the first and only time in her life.

In the archives of the Victoria & Albert Museum in South Kensington, London, there is a small ink drawing measuring 120mm by 145mm. In the drawing, three horses are pulling a plough up a hill, assisted by two farm labourers and followed by a cloud of birds, enticed by the freshly turned soil. This simple sketch was one of a number created by Potter when she wrote and illustrated *A Shortage of Horses*, a leaflet addressing the present shortage of horses in rural areas, with a warning about what might happen if war broke out and the horses were conscripted abroad. 'No doubt we should be paid for our horses,' she wrote, 'but what about our ruined crops?' Potter was a fierce campaigner on local conservation issues and she sent the leaflets out to contacts within the farming industry shortly after the government's re-election in 1910, but despite her efforts, thousands of horses were still dispatched over the next decade. Interestingly, Potter signed the leaflets: 'Yours Truly, North Country Farmer', and was desperate to keep her identity secret, insisting that 'it must not be let out the horse leaflet is written by a *female*'. In her lifetime, Potter protected large areas of the Lake District from development and, upon her death, bequeathed 4,000 acres of land and 15 farms and buildings to the National Trust. However, despite a lifetime of success in the fields of farming, conservation, literature and art, and an ambitious career in the face of a repressive, conservative upbringing, she still didn't believe women should have the vote, and publicly disapproved of the women's suffrage campaign.

For the horses that were conscripted, many would have been sent to places like the Catterick Garrison in North Yorkshire – a large establishment at the time, and now the biggest British Army base in the world. Following the outbreak of the First World War, a huge complex of stable blocks was built at Catterick, along with a top-of-the-range horse hospital, where the animals were prepared for their journey to the front line. Holding places like Catterick provided the calm before the storm of war; a space in which the horses were cared for and exercised, as well as being transformed from their former occupations as cab horses and farm ploughs into the warhorses that would bring so much brute strength to the Allied forces in France. And despite the original stable blocks no longer standing, recent archaeological work at Catterick has given an invaluable insight into what life was like for the warhorses in waiting. The equine barracks at Catterick were originally designed to house 40,000 horses, a huge number of animals that required stables, tack rooms, yards and exercise areas. Although the stables were demolished after the war, the infirmary building still stands, emblazoned with faded lettering on the outer wall, spelling 'Pharmacy', and is now home to the garrison's riding club. The old colic block still has sloping walls to help the horses get back to their feet, while the feed room still houses a huge safe, once used for the opiate medicines that would have been dispensed to wounded horses.

Most of the animals who left Catterick would have never returned to British soil. By the end of the war, only 62,000 horses had survived, and due to its recruitment drive, the army was left with far more horses than it would ever need during peacetime. Around 500,000 were sold for work, with 100,000 returning to Britain and the rest sent abroad. By this time, public concern had also been growing over how the horses were being treated, which meant the War Office was conducting investigations into every buyer, promising that unwanted horses would be destroyed rather than be sold to cruel owners. Around 61,000 of those who survived the war were considered unfit for work and ended up being sold for meat.

When the First World War did, at last, come to an end, there was still plenty of unrest in Europe that would eventually lead to another war, two decades later. So why were the horses dispersed instead of being kept ready and waiting for another likely conflict to break out? Aside from the number of casualties suffered by warhorses, there was another reason why they were no longer used in conflict after 1918. The invention of the tank is often said to have ended the First World War within a matter of weeks and while this isn't strictly true, it did turn the tide on the years of stalemate that had prevented either the German or Anglo-French armies claiming victory. Up until the tank's first use in the Battle of the Somme in 1916, the war had been characterised by sudden and brutal offensives, in which one side would break through the enemy's lines with massive artillery bombardments, followed by thousands of men attacking via no man's land. These offensives were not only incredibly costly and time-consuming but they also required the sacrifice of a huge number of soldiers who, in leaving the bunkers and shelters of the trenches to venture into no man's land, were then easy targets for machine guns that could shoot over long distances. A potential solution came from a handful of inventors who arrived at the same idea – to build an armed and armoured vehicle that could create gaps in the barbed wire fences surrounding the enemy's trenches, eliminate machine gun posts and bunkers, all the while protecting the infantry long enough for the defences to be breached and the trench captured.

The first model lumbered onto the battlefield in 1916. The Mark I model was British-designed and had been rushed into service, leading to many mechanical issues and the tanks being dark, noisy, hot and cramped. Added to this, the cannons and machine guns were positioned on either side, requiring the tank to fully turn in order to shoot in any given direction. Despite this and the fact it couldn't move much faster than a walking man, the tank was almost completely resistant to machine-gun fire. Later models were smaller and lighter, more comfortable, less cumbersome and enabled soldiers to take shelter as they walked behind them. As soon as they arrived on the Western Front, just the sight of them was enough to make several German strongpoints surrender; they even nicknamed them 'fire-breathing dragons'. Trench by trench, the German defences began to crumble. The war came to an end, but it was only the beginning of a new era of mechanised warfare, one that would play out all over again just a few years later in 1939 – with both sides taking advantage of the newest, and most violent, technology. Were a tank to face a horse and its rider, there would only be one winner. Horses began to be decommissioned from combat, although a small number would continue to fill supply and logistical roles.

U

Eight million horses were killed during the First World War, but they were not alone in their sacrifice. Animals have been used in conflict for centuries, in almost every war across the globe. Around 200,000 pigeons were used as messengers in the Second World War, and of the 17,000 parachuted into enemy territory, one in eight made it back home. Dogs are still routinely trained to hunt for mines and search for wounded soldiers. Mules were used as transport in the jungles of Burma (now Myanmar), with their vocal cords purposely damaged to keep them from making a noise. Camels, oxen and elephants were conscripted for similar purposes, while dolphins and sea lions are still trained today to search for underwater mines and to protect ships. Even the invertebrates paid their dues, with glow worms used in the First World War as an aid for map reading.

In 2004, the Animals in War Memorial was unveiled by the Princess Royal in London, just outside Hyde Park. It is marked with two inscriptions. The first reads: 'Animals in War. This monument is dedicated to all the animals that served and died alongside British and Allied forces in wars and campaigns throughout time.' And the second, much shorter inscription: 'They had no choice.' Designed by the sculptor David Backhouse, the memorial consists of a 58ft-long curved wall cut from Portland stone, carved with images of the animals that had been awarded the PDSA Dickin Medal – the animals' equivalent of the Victoria Cross – since the Second World War. On one side, two bronze mules struggle through a gap in the wall, heavily laden with equipment and clearly exhausted. Beyond the gap, however, a horse and a dog face north towards the park gardens, carrying nothing on their backs but hope; the dog appears to look back over its shoulder, as if bearing witness to the comrades they have lost.

Of the 60 animals that feature on the monument, 54 were commended for their service during the Second World War, including 32 pigeons, 18 dogs, one cat and three horses. On the centenary of the beginning of the First World War, 10 years after the memorial was unveiled, another horse was posthumously awarded the 66th Dickin Medal, on behalf of all the animals that served on the Western Front. Known as 'the horse the Germans couldn't kill', Warrior was a thoroughbred charger who served on the front line for the entire duration of the war, arriving in August 1914 and not coming home until Christmas 1918. During his service, he was subject to machine gun attacks by air, survived falling shells at the Battle of the Somme, was twice trapped under the burning beams of his stables, became buried under debris and almost sunk in the mud at Passchendaele. Through it all, he carried his owner General Jack Seely and helped to bring them both home to the Isle of Wight at the end of the war, where he lived with the family until his death in 1941, aged 32. According to those who fought alongside him, he frequently withstood shell fire even when explosions were going off in every direction; the soldiers who saw him said they felt empowered by his bravery, and that in his presence they too were able to face the horrors of the battlefield. In his obituary in *The Times* on 5 April 1941, General Seely remarked on his Warrior's fortitude in the field:

His escapes were quite wonderful. Again and again he survived when death seemed certain and, indeed, befell all his neighbours. It was not all hazard; sometimes it was due to his intelligence. I have seen him, even when a shell has burst within a few feet, stand still without a tremor – just turn his head and, unconcerned, look at the smoke of the burst.

Warrior was one of the millions of animals who had no choice but to carry their soldiers into battle and brave the war as best they could. Their services may not be as well remembered as their human counterparts, but each year on Armistice Day, somebody might place a ring of purple poppies on the Cenotaph, chosen to commemorate the often forgotten non-human victims of war. The stories of Britain's warhorses have gone on to inspire countless books, films, plays and poems, including *War Horse* by Michael Morpurgo, the 1982 novel adapted to both film and a successful theatre production, about a conscripted horse called Joey and his journey to war and back again. More renowned in his own time, the war poet Henry Chappell also captured the traumatic experiences these horses went through, along with the bond they formed with their riders along the way. In his poem 'A Soldier's Kiss', the final moments of a mortally wounded horse are witnessed by his soldier who, under shot and shell, risks his own life to kneel by his dying companion's side:

Only a dying horse! Pull off the gear,
And slip the needless bit from frothing jaws,
Drag it aside there, leaving the roadway clear –
The battery thunders on with scarce a pause.

Prone by the shell-swept highway there it lies
With quivering limbs, as fast the life tide fails,
Dark films are closing o'er the faithful eyes
That mutely plead for aid where none avails.

Onward the battery roll, but one there speeds,
Heedlessly of comrade's voice or bursting shell,
Back to the wounded friend who lonely bleeds
Beside the stony highway where it fell.

Only a dying horse! He swiftly kneels,
Lifts the limp head and hears the shivering sigh
Kisses his friend, while down his cheek there steals
Sweet pity's tear: 'Goodbye Old Man, Goodbye.'

No honours wait him, Medal, Badge or Star,
Though scarce could war a kindlier deed unfold;
He bears within his breast, more precious far
Beyond the gift of kings, a heart of gold.

CHAPTER ELEVEN

The Herd

I wasn't sure what to expect when I arrived at the estate on an overcast afternoon in March. I knew it was a place like no other – a place as close to wild as it is possible to be in the south of England, at least. My imagination had therefore conjured up something like a National Trust property from a dystopian future, like in H. G. Wells' *The Time Machine* when he springs forward to the year 802,701, and all the magnificent buildings of the past have deteriorated into nothing. I knew there was a castle here somewhere, and I couldn't help wondering if that, too, had been surrendered to nature, overthrown by ivy and insects and gorse. The reality was that when I turned off the main road and rattled over the cattle grid, it didn't seem too different at first glance. In fact, it was quiet, which was unsurprising for both the time of day and the season. I discovered later that one disgruntled Facebook user had even complained that there were 'no animals' here, despite it being the home of the most famous safaris in Sussex. I could see their point, I suppose. There were no animals wandering in front of my car or flying low over the road before me, but that, of course, was the whole point. This place was not just for us. It was not designed to please the human eye, but to be a sanctuary for every other species that might be lucky enough to stumble upon it.

As it happened, I was not in the pages of a dystopian novel but at the Knepp Estate in West Sussex, just south of Horsham. The chances that you will have heard of Knepp already are high. It has become the Graceland of UK conservation, a beacon for anyone weighed down by the burden of ecological crisis and who desperately wants to find a different way forward. The story of Knepp is one that is, by now, familiar to many: a castle; a farm; an inheritance, and a forward-thinking couple willing to let go of the past and take a risk on the future. It's the sort of conservation success story you almost don't want to look directly at, in case it really is too good to be true and vanishes like a dream at first light. I had been waiting to come here for years, and the day had finally come. Thick mud, grey sky, leafless trees and thorny scrub in every direction. What could have been mistaken for an abandoned battlefield was, in fact, quite the opposite. It was a paradise.

The story of the Knepp Estate can be traced back to the twelfth century, when the old Knepp Castle was first built as a hunting lodge. The remains of this ruin are still visible today, taking the form of a single tower on a grassy mound next to the A24. When the estate first came into the hands of the Burrell family, a second castle was commissioned by the Regency architect John Nash, and it was this building and the surrounding 3,500 acres of land that the present owner, Charlie Burrell, inherited from his grandparents in 1987. Together with his wife, the writer Isabella Tree, they renovated the house and set to work on the land. Having trained at agricultural college, Charlie expected to continue the farming tradition at Knepp, but the unpalatable truth was that the farm had been losing money for decades and despite attempts to modernise and diversify, they were unable to make a sustainable profit. In February 2000, Charlie and Isabella made the decision to sell their dairy herds and farm machinery, and put the arable land out to contract, clearing their debts but leaving them with an uncertain future.

The main issue with running the estate was the land itself, which was simply not conducive to the modern practice of intensive farming. The estate is located in an area known as the Low Weald, a quintessentially medieval landscape characterised by low-lying clay vales and gentle ridges of limestone and sandstone. At Knepp, the clay in particular means the soil is like concrete in summer, so dry and deeply cracked you can sometimes put your whole arm into the ground and come out clean. And in winter, the ground had been described as 'unfathomable porridge', with most machines unable to even drive across the fields in the worst months. They tried for 17 years to make the estate commercially viable, but, outcompeted by larger, more industrialised farms with better soils, it was time to think differently.

Charlie and Isabella were aware of the historical changes that had been happening to the landscape since the Second World War, when the 'Dig for Victory' campaign turned swathes of land into agricultural spaces. When the war ended, this practice continued, together with the introduction of chemical fertilisers, pesticides, modern machinery and new varieties of crops – and the age of intensive farming began. In exchange for all this extra productivity, however, and despite the fact that nobody needed this much food (even today, we waste 40 per cent globally of all the food we produce), the environmental damage was devastating. In the last few decades of the twentieth century, anecdotal observations turned to scientific studies, and the whisperings of what we were doing to the landscape became undeniable truths. The barely regulated rise of intensive farming was leading to what the environmentalist Rachel Carson termed a 'silent spring', a world devoid of insect populations and the entire food chains that survived off them. Not only was this catastrophic for the natural world, but as we have been so slow to understand, our species was part of that world, too, which meant our own future was looking just as dark.

In 2002, Knepp received funding to restore an area of 350 acres in the middle of the estate that had been under the plough since the Second World War. The restoration was successful, and they considered the possibility of turning the entire estate into a conservation project, one that was led by natural processes that allowed nature to take the driving seat. This idea would later become commonly known as 'rewilding', and with the support of other ecologists, landowners and communities exploring the same idea around the world, they successfully applied for government support to establish a 'Biodiverse Wilderness Area' on their land.

Knepp has since become a beacon for the conservation movement, experimenting and sharing their work with the ecological world, and most astonishingly of all, seeing the entire landscape transform before their eyes. The biggest change the team implemented was putting grazing animals back into the landscape, in place of the megafauna that would have once roamed here, and so driving a new form of hands-off habitat creation that had seen the local wildlife population explode. Longhorn cattle were brought in as a proxy for the aurochs that would have once roamed here (now extinct), while the Exmoor ponies and Tamworth pigs joined the red, fallow and roe deer populations to replicate the sort of animals that existed together here centuries ago. In doing so, the mosaic of habitats created by different grazing patterns had brought an abundance of wildlife back to Knepp, some species of which hadn't been seen here in living memory. Not only did they return, but extremely rare species like turtle doves, nightingales, peregrine falcons and purple emperor butterflies had now started breeding here, too – and all, incredibly, within 20 miles of Gatwick airport.

Ask anyone with a vague interest in nature, particularly rewilding, and they are likely to have heard of Knepp – and that very much included me. I had been desperate to visit for years, but for one reason or another, this was the first time I had made the journey, despite it being only an hour from my house. I arrived, stretched my legs and tap-tapped a message to Rina Quinlan, the wildlife guide and researcher who had kindly agreed to show me around. Rina's interests were in rewilding, reintroductions and large herbivores, which made her the perfect person to interrogate about the animals I had come here to see – the herd of Exmoor ponies that had been introduced to Knepp a few years ago and whose hoofprints we were now following through the thick, clay clods underfoot, stopping now and then to admire the white storks nesting in a tree above our heads, another species flourishing on the estate.

As we walked together, Rina pointed out that we were travelling along a herbivore highway; this stretch of soft, wet ground was speckled with hoofprints from the horses and cattle, as well as snout marks where the pigs had been rooting for grubs. We were tracking the hoofprints to find out where one of the two Exmoor pony herds might be that afternoon. 'The horses are habitual,' Rina explained, 'so I have an idea of where they might be, but it's always worth checking for fresh prints. They have a huge expanse of land to explore, but these ponies tend to keep themselves to a smaller home range.' The herd we were looking for was made up of 13 non-breeding females, all mothers and daughters, ranging in age between eight and 24. We started splodging slowly and carefully through the mud and shrubbery, weaving our way through the unique landscape that was Knepp estate. It was like nowhere I'd ever been – undoubtedly beautiful, but certainly not in the usual sense you might think of when you imagine nature reserves. In most directions, all we could see were gorse bushes, or 'furze'. And as we had not quite entered the lighter half of the year, the warmth of spring was still held back and the gorse had not yet fallen into its full blossoms of bright, coconut-scented yellow. Instead, it was a mass of thorns, not unlike the image that surrounded the fairy-tale castles of my childhood, into which a knight might have to venture to rescue a damsel. Together with the mud, the lack of paths and signposts, the hotchpotch of trees and shrubs that had clearly not been organised by human hands, this place felt unfamiliar in its chaos, and I realised how little real wilderness

I had experienced in my life, particularly growing up in the south of England where it's difficult to find anywhere out of earshot of a busy motorway. Despite nearly having my boot sucked off by the clay puddles at least three times, I relished the newness of this place. I recognised the plants and the birds, the rousing sensation of late winter and the sounds of the world waking up. But there was something in the air here that felt so different, it was almost exotic.

I asked Rina how she ended up working in a place like this: 'I've been passionate about nature all my life,' she told me. 'But ecology had not been my career path of choice until recently. I loved horses as a child, and worked a few jobs when I was younger on a dealer's yard, then a racecourse, and then for an equestrian magazine on the marketing team. After a stint of travelling, I then landed a job with an equestrian concierge firm, organising riding trips for affluent clients, from polo to hunting and everything in between, in locations all around the world. I was exposed to horses, riding and travel all the time – three of my favourite things – but I realised I was working in a world I didn't really believe in.' After returning from a horseback safari in Africa, where she experienced the wilderness and magic of the African landscape, Rina found London and her job too jarring. Feeling like she was stuck in a rut and not sure what to do, she returned to her other passion – being outdoors in nature and caring for the world we live in. Leaving her job and salary behind, she enrolled in an Open University degree in environmental science, and it was around this time that she read one of the books that brought rewilding to mainstream audiences – *Feral* by George Monbiot. This, she joked, was what lots of conservationists referred to as the 'gateway drug' to rewilding. She was fascinated by the idea, and having grown up in Sussex and been familiar with the Knepp project, she joined the safari team and went from there, working as a rewilding consultant with a focus on large herbivores.

The conversation turned to each other as we wandered through this new world. Rina and I were close in age and both mothers to young daughters, which meant the subject, as it always does, drifted to that most life-changing of experiences – becoming a parent. But it wasn't completely off topic. In fact, the discussion soon returned to the estate's animals again, for what are we but animals ourselves? We talked about the power of aligning ourselves with our natural instincts and intuitions, how much more enjoyable life can be when we do so, and how much calmer the waters of motherhood are to navigate. Rina had found becoming a mother had enriched her experience observing the ponies so closely, particularly as the herd we were now following was made up exclusively of mothers and daughters. It was almost impossible to observe their relationships without empathising, wholeheartedly, with their maternal behaviours, their instincts, desires and fears. It is something you can't unsee – just as everything is viewed through a different lens, for better or worse, when you step into parenthood.

While discussing familiar relationships within the herd, Rina was reminded of not only watching the Knepp ponies, but in caring for her own horses at home, too. 'There aren't many opportunities in the world to watch a real herd of wild horses being able to fully express their natural behaviours, but as the herds settled in and found the freedom to live as they pleased, I began to think differently about our entire relationship with domestic horses.' One of the things she had learnt from watching the herds was about dominance. 'We often think of a herd of horses having a dominant male or a dominant female, but through watching the ponies on the estate, there doesn't seem to be "dominance" in that way – only a kind of older wisdom, although I realise that's anthropomorphising it a bit,' she said, smiling. 'Wild herds have even been known to have subordinate males. There might be two males keeping a lookout like sentries, possibly even allowed to mate with some of the mares, although obviously not as much as the most dominant male in the herd. In a traditional stable setting, the reason a horse might seem aggressive isn't necessarily down to a question of dominance, but more likely a sense of scarcity around food. In the wild, there is no scarcity for individuals – either the whole herd eats, or nobody eats. But in a stable, one horse can have a bulging hay net while another won't be fed for another hour. It creates tension that doesn't really exist in the wild.' She went on to explain that, despite the Hollywood image of wild stallions rearing and fighting, wild horses are unlikely to waste precious energy fighting among themselves, except for the odd bicker. 'Stallions can fight between themselves over females if they feel inclined, but studies have shown that when mares have a range of mates to choose from, they will often go for "kinder", more gentle stallions, even if they have fought – and lost – to another.'

Watching the herd through a mother's eyes has also helped shape her observations, particularly in the light of how we form relationships with our own children. There are so many rules that new mothers feel obliged to follow, most of which are based on cultural norms rather than biological ones: we must breastfeed, but not for too long; we must leave our children to cry or they will become spoilt; we must create rigid routines for eating, playing and sleeping. None of these rules are seen in the natural world but we have somehow convinced ourselves they are necessary to raise a healthy child, and in watching the pony herds, Rina felt more than ever that we have pushed our domesticated horses too far into this rigid way of living, too. In a 'natural' herd, there is no rush to wean the young from their mares, no forced cut-off point to separate a mother from her daughter. Siblings have strong relationships, too, which is something that has been lost from domesticated horses as they are separated from their siblings so early on. 'I would love to see horses treated more like dogs,' she explained. 'Dogs are generally kept with one family, in one home, for life, quite often with a sibling or at least a family unit around them. Horses can be moved from owner to owner, yard to yard, several times in just one lifetime. I would love to see horses weaned later than the usual six months, to see them have homes for life and kept in a familiar herd.'

Another idea coming through in research circles is that of a natal band – a new term that is helping to reframe outdated ideas about dominance and aggression. 'Many researchers would now consider this herd to be a natal band, rather than a stallion–led hareem,' Rina told me. 'You could almost see it like a female commune. And when mothers and older siblings are too busy to play with the young colts, the stallions will often take that role, teaching them through play. With normal domesticated horses, stallions are rarely, if ever, given the opportunity to spend time with their babies, and we can see from watching this herd that it isn't natural for them to be separated like that. We don't always think about the social dynamics of herbivores, but horses have particularly strong matrilineal relationships. If their daughters are kicked out of a herd, mothers have been known to move on with them. But in the equestrian industry, horses are weaned and sold very young, moved around all the time, and have less of a chance to form a natural bond with a herd, or even with another horse, for any length of time. I've known some livery owners to even move their horses around on purpose to stop them forming too close friendships, which just shows how much we tend to put our own needs first.' Rina also explained how most horses aren't even allowed to express themselves when it comes to mourning. 'If a livestock animal dies at Knepp, it has to be removed under current regulations. But if you look at elephants in the wild, who also live in tight, sociable herds, they mourn their dead, and will even revisit old sites where a herd mate died, just as we would visit a grave. Not only are there psychological benefits to this behaviour which horses and other livestock are denied, it is also a waste of the nutrients that should naturally pass back to the earth. Surely it makes sense for the animals to return to the soil that fed and nurtured them all their lives?'

We clomped a little further through the clay and rounded a corner into another muddy bog, where I became so intent on not losing my welly, I almost didn't spot the herd gathered at the far end of the field. There they stood, this cluster of chocolate brown ponies, whose coats shone, beneath flecks of clay, in a rainbow of smudgy dark colours; ink black, plum brown, and in the forelocks, streaks of dun like saffron threads. They were smaller than I had imagined – only about 12 horse hands – and Rina laughed when she told me that archaeological records suggest these tiny ponies were actually used by the Romans for cavalry soldiers, meaning the Hollywood depictions of warriors galloping along on huge stallions is a bit of a stretch. Curious and friendly, but with the streetwise, half-feral attitudes that differentiate them from tame horses, these were beautiful, happy animals – and clearly, I realised as clay-tinted water began trickling through a hole in my boot, much better suited to this magical wilderness than I was.

The herd began to move across the field and through the hedgerow, and we followed slowly behind, watching every intricacy of their interactions; I could see why Rina was so addicted to observing them. One rolled, and several more followed suit. Another urinated, and all of a sudden half the herd was peeing together. Everything about them was joyful to witness. In the next field, joining a herd of longhorn cattle relaxing in the afternoon light, the ponies cantered together in a dark conga line of rumps, hooves and forelocks. And then they stopped, and stood together, perfectly still – watching us with curious eyes as we drifted closer. From here, lined up along the summit of the hill, it was easy to see why the Exmoors had been chosen to take the place of the megafauna that once roamed here, thousands of years ago. Their stockiness, mealy muzzles and rounded bellies were almost identical to the Palaeolithic portraits of their ancestors, those secret paintings on the cave walls of Lascaux. And although they were genetically different to the European wild horse, Rina suspected there was more work to be done to discover just how closely connected these modern ponies were to their wild ancestors.

U

Exmoors are only one of the many native breeds of free-roaming pony in the UK, but together with Dartmoors and New Forests, they are certainly some of the best known to the general public. There are, however, a surprising number of other native breeds in almost every corner of the country, not only shaped by the habitats in which they have adapted and thrived, but shaping those same landscapes themselves in return. Few people know more about these breeds than Ruth Chamberlain (known online as 'Ruth on the Hoof'), a photographer and writer who grew up surrounded by horses, from watching the fell ponies in the Lake District to learning to ride on a little partbred Welsh mountain pony. After years of observing native breeds and their unique characteristics, she decided to start photographing the breeds she could find around Britain and Ireland and is writing a book to document the project. 'It came about as part of a little project I started online,' she said. 'I used to post images of fell ponies in local visitor groups on social media, and I was shocked at how little people knew about the breed. I realised it was the same throughout most of the UK, so I decided I wanted to showcase these breeds in their natural environment. Sharing photographs of ponies in familiar landscapes was incredibly popular with the general public, and through the project I have also started to talk about how these ponies shape their local landscapes, too. Most of our native breeds are rare and at risk, but they are such a huge part of our heritage and it would be such a loss if they died out. The book, and the project as a whole, is all about educating people about our native breeds while also promoting them and making people aware of their existence.'

Like the Exmoors at Knepp, native pony breeds are valuable in their own right, but they can also play a vital role in a sustainable, more environmentally conscious future. Most have a hardy stature, good teeth and small, sharp feet, often selectively grazing on the sweet but swiftly growing young shoots of gorse, purple moor grass, soft rush, brambles and thistles, as well as trampling bracken. Not only do they break down taller vegetation but they also graze close to the ground, leaving bare patches for butterflies and other pollinators. 'Equines are native to the UK,' explained Ruth, 'and wild horses existed in Europe long after the last Ice Age, which is made up of similar habitats to the UK. This suggests that equines have always been an integral part of the native fauna of this country. And compared with other herbivores like cattle and deer, ponies are unique in their grazing behaviour. They have upper incisors and a prehensile lip which allows them to neatly and delicately bite plants – a bit like pruning. And any gardener can tell you the importance of pruning to keep plants healthy. It is a totally natural mechanism and horses fill the role perfectly, which means they can be hugely beneficial to the environment, especially in many of the ecosystems here in the UK that need this type of grazing to nurture a balanced and sustainable habitat.'

As with all conservation grazing schemes in which megafauna are (re)introduced to an area in order to influence the habitat, there are those who claim the damage caused by overgrazing can outweigh any benefits. Overgrazing can compact and degrade grassland, erode the soil, prevent plants from flowering, encourage poaching and reduce habitat variation; undergrazing, too, can allow coarse grasses and shrubs to grow too high and decrease less competitive species. The key for landowners is to create a manageable grazing programme, carefully adapted to the breed and quantity of herbivores, as well as ensuring the movement of their livestock is suitably timed and rotated. Despite some opposition, research shows that well-managed grazing schemes provide huge benefits for wildlife, people and the landscape as a whole; today, carefully planned grazing schemes are in use by most of the UK's landowning conservation organisations.

Native ponies can be found all over the UK, but when they are not documented and protected properly, it can lead to a breed's extinction. The Galloway pony, for example, was once native to Scotland and northern England where it was prized for its resilience and ability to travel long distances in harsh conditions. Not well suited to farm work, Galloways were crossbred to produce a more versatile animal, used for border raids, to drive cattle and to haul lead ore. Unfortunately, this crossbreeding diluted the bloodline, and by the eighteenth century the breed was quickly becoming absorbed into the fell pony. By 1814, one agricultural report confirmed the Galloways were 'almost lost':

> The province of Galloway formerly possessed a breed of horses peculiar to itself, which were in high estimation for the saddle, being, though of a small size, exceedingly hardy and active ... The soils of Galloway, in their unimproved state, are evidently adapted for rearing such a breed of horses; and in the moors and mountainous part of the country, a few of the native breed are still to be found ... Such as have a considerable portion of the old blood are easily distinguished by their smallness of head and neck, and cleanness of bone.

Within a few decades, the Galloway was considered an extinct breed – a warning of what could happen to any of our native breeds if they are not documented and protected.

For Ruth and many others, it is vital to care for these ponies if we want to preserve the heritage of our landscapes. 'Individual breeds hold so much cultural value within the wider context of our country's history,' she explained. 'Take the hill farmers of the Lake District and their fell ponies – a breed perfectly adapted for life on the fells. The ground is often rocky and steep and the fell pony moves in such a way as to make it seem effortless. Similarly, the Highland pony moves in a way more suited to life in the mountains. I have also noticed other adaptations in each breed that seem to reflect their environment. The Exmoor ponies have "toad eyes" to protect them from the rain as, generally speaking, they do not have long manes that would typically do the same job. But in the Lake District, the fell ponies tend to grow much longer manes, tails and coats, as they are often exposed to drastically harsh and changeable weather, and seem to have adapted to be able to tolerate it better. I also find that breeds like the Highland pony, which comes from a notoriously poor area in terms of vegetation, tend to gain lots of weight when they come further south to "richer" pastures – another example of how these breeds have been so perfectly adapted to their local habitats, managed by the people who have lived and worked alongside them in the same harsh conditions for centuries.'

Native ponies on the whole have become a treasured part of our national landscape, but it is just as important to recognise the individual breeds found in each area, as they tell so many stories about the history of Britain's people and places. 'Protecting these ponies,' explained Ruth, 'means we protect our cultural history and the links we have to past communities. In doing so, we will also have more resilient ponies that require less attention and management, making them a more sustainable choice. Documenting these breeds is so important because of the extreme pressures being put on them, as well as the misinformation about how they graze. Sadly, some organisations still do not understand the benefits of horses and want them removed from the land – which would be devastating for the ponies and their local communities, as well as the biodiversity that thrives in their wake.'

U

On the Knepp estate, Rina shares her knowledge of rewilding and megafauna as a consultant, and is often asked about which breeds are best for projects like these. 'In my opinion, and based on scientific research, any horse – not even just the native breeds – can be used for rewilding,' she explained. 'Natives can certainly be better adapted to certain environments, but you can see from the Australian brumbies and American mustangs that even "high-quality" horses can go feral and thrive in free-roaming herds.' But she also theorised why native breeds might still be the superior choice: 'If you can pick and choose which breeds to use for rewilding, there is a lot to be said for selecting culturally appropriate ones – those which have a historical connection to the area, are well suited physically, and are treasured by local communities. Fell ponies for the Lake District; New Forests for Hampshire heathlands; Welsh ponies for the Cambrian mountains. The reason is that it helps people connect with the idea of rewilding in general, as they tend to already have a positive view of their local ponies, and are therefore more likely to support an expansion of the local population in the name of biodiversity.'

Rina also mentioned a primitive horse breed that is known for dividing opinion in the UK, despite being perfectly suited to its role in conservation grazing. The rare and hardy konik pony is a breed native to Poland, and one of those chosen by Lutz Heck in his failed attempt to backbreed the tarpan. I was particularly familiar with the apparent controversy of this breed because I once wrote an article for a magazine about conservation grazing ponies, and made the bold move of mentioning koniks as one of the breeds that are used in grazing projects across the UK. It enraged one reader so much that they felt obliged to write me an angry letter claiming koniks shouldn't even be mentioned in the same breath as our native ponies. It took me by surprise because in terms of scientific evidence on koniks in the UK – which should surely be the most important factor – they appear to fare just as well as our own breeds; I could only conclude the reader was a Eurosceptic. Koniks are particularly well suited to places like Wicken Fen in Cambridgeshire, the National Trust's oldest nature reserve and one of Europe's most important wetlands. There are more than 9,000 species thriving on the reserve, living among the flowering meadows, sedge and reedbeds, as well as grazing Highland cattle and konik ponies. The koniks were deliberately chosen because they originate from similar lowland habitats in eastern Europe; they were brought in as part of a 100-year-long project to expand the fen to a size of 22 square miles. The ponies are excellent at creating new wetland habitats through their grazing patterns, rolling hollows, piles of dung, and the pockets of water formed by their hoofprints, all of which support large numbers of flies, snails, spiders and beetles that strengthen the local ecosystem from the ground up.

For Rina, she welcomes any breed into the world of rewilding, but using native breeds means it is easier to get the public on board. They look the part and are well adapted to their environment, which means you can also weave cultural stories into their role in our future landscapes. She is also wary of some native pony societies being too strict with what 'counts' as a particular breed, which can sometimes mean a pony is stripped of its pedigree for having a white streak in its coat, or the wrong conformation. While she is keen to protect native breeds across the country, she would also like to look into crossbreeding for conservation grazing purposes. 'The good news,' she told me, 'is that demand for these horses for rewilding and conservation projects is only increasing. Whenever we need to remove a stallion or another horse from the herd for reasons of genetic diversity, for example, there is always somewhere for them to move to, which wasn't the case not so long ago.'

Leaving the ponies to the apricot glow of the late winter afternoon, we walked back through the fields and shrubs of the estate. There was something to look at in every direction; so many loose and untamed plants that I was unused to seeing in the manicured landscapes of Britain. In the trees above, we heard the clattering call of white storks as they circled their nests, looking every bit like pterodactyls from my ground-level view. Rina told me that strange clattering noise, made by tapping their bills together, was the way they communicated during courtship, as well as sounding the alarm for predators or other storks nearby. It was unearthly to listen to, like an audio mash-up of *Predator*, *The Grudge* and *Jurassic Park*. But even more astonishing was the fact that a healthy population of these birds might be seen in their hundreds; I couldn't begin to imagine what that might sound like. White storks might not be the first species we think of in British rewilding, but there is significant evidence to show they were once a breeding bird here, with an archaeological record stretching back 360,000 years; just outside the nearby town of Worthing, Storrington village was originally named Estorchestone by the Saxons, which means 'the village of the storks'. Like almost everything that made its home at Knepp, the storks were breeding successfully and had a bright, noisy future here among the treetops. They had already lined their nests with dried horse dung for insulation, and their presence was almost guaranteed to have a positive influence on the other species; in one study of European storks, there were three tree sparrow nests found nestled within a single stork nest.

'The thorn is the mother of the oak,' so goes the ancient forestry saying, rooted in a time before green plastic tubes became tree planting tools and when thorny shrubs were encouraged to grow beside oak saplings to protect them in their youth. Thorny scrub was once so highly valued that a 1768 statute in New Forest law imposed three months of forced labour to anyone found removing it. Everywhere I looked at Knepp there were tangles of hawthorn, blackthorn, elder and bramble, and hidden inside were young, healthy trees, cautiously protected like damsels in a castle, waiting to break free into the sunlight. Elsewhere, trenches of top soil had been turned over by grub-seeking pig snouts, who were here to act as a proxy for wild boar. Their snuffling helped open the earth up to new seeds and plants, enriching the soil and providing sun traps for insects like mining bees. The ecosystems that had evolved around the ponies at Knepp were also fascinating, as Rina explained to me: 'There are species living here that are almost entirely dependent on the ponies' presence. When the violet dor beetle was found here a few years ago – a species that loves horse dung – it was the first recorded sighting in Sussex for 50 years. And we have a species of lesser earwig that feeds on the mycelia of moulds found on horse dung, too.' Elsewhere, chough reintroduction projects along coastal grazing plains rely on healthy, chemical-free herbivore populations nearby, simply because of the invertebrates contained in their dung.

Perhaps it was the weight of a lifetime of eco-anxiety, but wandering through the wilderness of the Knepp estate felt so healing that I almost didn't want to breathe in case I broke the spell. In a world where we face a diminishing abundance of biodiversity daily, it was bizarre to be in a place – even a small one – where numbers were going up and not down, where life was being created instead of destroyed. But it also raised the larger question of what true wilderness really meant – how do we label it, and who decides what it looks like? And that was the beauty of working to rewild a damaged world – there was no room for black-and-white thinking. 'One of the exciting things about rewilding,' explained Rina, 'is that it teaches you not to see things so rigidly. You can be more flexible, more adaptable. And with climate change happening anyway, ecosystems are changing all the time, so what baselines do we realistically have to work with?' We can argue all day about whether a species is native or not, or which breed is better for which role. But the most important lesson that Rina seems to have learnt from rewilding is the need to let go of our control over the world around us. 'We want horses to stay wild, and yet we also want to dominate them,' she observed. Perhaps it was time to stop viewing the world through such an anthropocentric lens, and to start embracing this more beautiful and interconnected reality of what the landscape could really look like.

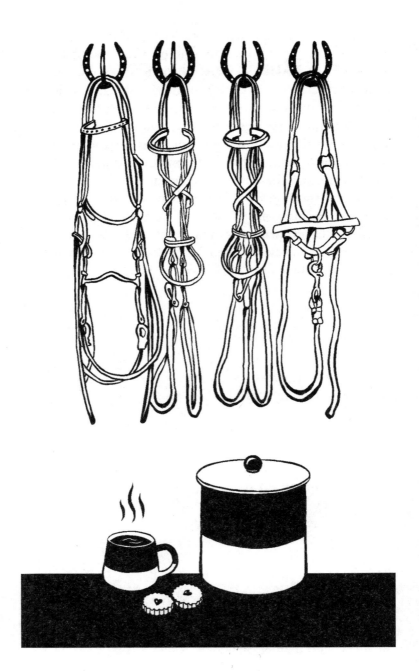

CHAPTER TWELVE

The Go-Between

The velvet nub of a horse's nose is magical. That rounded snout with a slight softness between the nostrils, coated in such fine hair that it draws your knuckles in like a magnet, searching for a light embrace. It is the part closest to the mouth, of course, so to reach out and touch it is to accept the risk of having your fingers nibbled. But it's worth it for the fuzz. The writer and animal rights campaigner John Galsworthy once said: 'there is nothing alive quite so beautiful as a horse'. And when you stand before one after a ride and watch it chew hay with half-closed, long-lashed eyes, it's easy to agree with him. The anatomical beauty of horses has drawn our attention for centuries – that perfect combination of wildness and wisdom, the desire for sunlight and freedom and wide open plains, combined with a fondness for carrots and human contact. Wild or domesticated, there is simply no animal like it.

One bright afternoon in January, I found myself running a comb through the forelock of a small, grey pony called Peanut. At my feet, my daughter Olive was attempting to brush his leg. The weather was beautiful; warm sunshine, daffodils sprouting up by the gate, and a flock of sparrows chittering by the stable door where my mother-in-law Chris kept her New Forest pony, Sparkle. She had been taking Olive up to the yard every week since she turned one, and thanks to the kind lady who kept Peanut there, too, Olive had been able to sit on him and bob about the yard, brush his coat, feed him hay, and enjoy the mud and puddles and biscuits that came along with equestrian life.

We finished grooming Peanut, tacked him up, popped Olive's cycling helmet on and lifted her into the saddle. Her little legs were too short for the stirrups, so we wedged them into the gap above and gave her the lead rope to hold in her mittened hands, looped around Peanut's neck like reins. She smiled and sat upright, ready for an adventure, and we clicked the pony into a gentle walk. I stayed beside her in case she fell, but she was now so used to the saddle that she had relaxed into her seat, safe and sturdy, pointing around her with joy at the moon ('moo!'), the chickens ('cheekee!') and the other horses ('hose!'). Two red kites and a buzzard circled above us, waltzing to the *tink tink tink* of the farrier as he worked outside the stables. We clip-clopped out of the gate and along the green lanes, listening to the birds singing in the woods, then back again to the yard as the sun began to set, where Olive returned to the ground and we bid good evening to Peanut with a net full of hay.

The kettle was boiled and we sat among the paint-flaked walls, misshapen horseshoes and drying numnahs of the tack room, the cosiest place to be after a winter's ride. I spotted an old swallow's nest in the rafters that would soon be alive with young, the offspring of birds that were readying themselves for the long journey back from Africa, across land and sea, chasing the sun. I cradled my coffee, breathed in the smell of warm horse and leather and felt all the peace and hope of life rolled out before me.

Over the last few centuries, the societal roles of Britain's horses have changed dramatically, from jousting steeds to weapons of war, apple millers to carriage pullers. Where there has been a demand for power, horses have stepped in to supply it, and as a consequence, our landscape has shifted and been shaped to facilitate the needs of equines. But now there are cars instead of carriages, and electricity instead of horsepower. Even the warhorses have been cast aside to make way for newer, darker breeds of weaponry. So what lies ahead for the horses of Britain, Europe and beyond? Their uses may have changed, but horses are far from redundant in the modern world. Instead of relying on their labour, we now value them for their ability to graze nature reserves, run races, jump fences and carry us from one bridleway to another in the spirit of recreation. But there is still more to their story that goes beyond the familiar touchstones of twenty-first-century equestrianism, particularly when we look outside the stable yard and into the broader spheres of health, fitness and wellbeing.

Horse riding is a deceptively exhausting hobby. It is easy to watch a rider sitting astride their horse and imagine the latter is doing most of the work but as with everything equestrian, it is a collaborative effort. Even the gentlest walk or trot requires good core muscles to stay balanced, and strong inner thighs and pelvic muscles to maintain a good posture and position. One BHS-commissioned study found that just half an hour of horse-related activity, such as mucking out, grooming, carrying buckets, moving hay bales and lifting saddles onto the back of a horse, is classed as moderate exercise and can reduce the risk of cardiovascular disease by up to 35 per cent. A medium-length ride with plenty of trotting and a few canters can burn several hundred calories, not to mention competitive sports like show jumping, cross country and dressage. Like swimming, you often don't realise how much you have exerted yourself until you're scrambling out of the saddle, jelly-legged, flush-faced and desperate to eat something sweet and carb-based.

Aside from the physical benefits, horse riding is catching the interest of more practitioners and academics in the medical field, particularly a newer concept known as equine-assisted psychotherapy. What happens during a session is determined by the individuals' needs, but patients are generally invited to spend time with one or more horses to understand how they interact and to see whether it opens up new channels of communication to which the human language does not always have access. There are many equine therapy facilities around the country, including Operation Centaur, a clinic based in Richmond Park on the edge of London. I spoke to Dr Andreas Liefooghe, a lifelong horseman, chartered psychologist and founding director of the project, to find out what he had learnt from this innovative form of therapy.

'For many people,' Dr Liefooghe explained, 'therapy is about language. Language is how something that's inside of us can come to the outside, and that's how therapy works, really. That is what Freud referred to as the "talking cure". We have something inside of us that we can't necessarily identify – a feeling or a pressure – and it is only when we can put that feeling into words that we can release it because we can share it, and other people can help us understand it. That's the basic principle of therapy. But what do you do if people can't or won't talk? As a therapist, you're stuck. And this is where horses come in. Horses are masters of communication, and yet they don't speak in what we would recognise as a language. Instead, we have to figure out how to connect with them, and in doing so, we can then reconnect with ourselves.' This non-verbal language holds the key: it is how humans communicated before we developed language as we know it today, or as Dr Liefooghe referred to it, 'the most sophisticated cultural artefact we have'. As newborns, we are not preloaded with language, only the ability to acquire it during our lifetime. It is a cultural acquisition rather than a natural one. In contrast, the way horses communicate with each other is purely natural. This makes it so powerful in equine therapy: 'We have unlearnt the non-verbal communication that horses and other animals have access to,' Dr Liefooghe continued, 'so we do not always trust it at first. But for people who don't want to talk, such as those who have suffered trauma or PTSD, people on the autistic spectrum, teenagers and older children, or others who have simply had their fill of talking therapy and feel like they need something more, they often try equine therapy and find they are then able to talk more openly about their feelings. There is no magic in our sessions – the horses don't wear feathers on their heads or jump through flaming hoops. It is simple, experiential, on-the-ground work, but it is powerful.' One of the groups, Project Centaur, works with prisons and their inmates. Dr Liefooghe found that equine therapy helped several of the prisoners reconnect with the concept of hope; the bond they formed with the horses brought back happy memories of childhood and time with their parents, reminding them that life is not all doom and gloom, and it helped to break negative thought cycles.

When I asked what inspired Dr Liefooghe to set up Operation Centaur, he explained that he had been a horseman all his life, but he took a break from horses while living and studying in central London. But despite his career moving further towards psychology and academia, he found that horses were still there, always at the back of his mind: 'I was then given an opportunity to reconnect with horses within the realms of my academic field, and I immediately sensed there was a way to draw horses further into my psychological work. Despite resisting the idea for a while and trying to keep my work and equestrian life separate, the two kept converging. There wasn't a huge amount going on in the UK in this field, however, so I visited Germany, Denmark and California to find out more from other groups who were investigating it. It wasn't until I met a woman called StarrLee Heady, who was working just north of Miami, that I got a sense of how it all worked. She had been working with Navy SEALs who had returned from Iraq and Afghanistan and was seeing positive results through equine therapy sessions. At the time, there was a shortage of solid evidence around the practice, so I decided to start collecting qualitative data and mapping out how this could become a fully-fledged psychotherapeutic intervention. In 2012, Operation Centaur formally welcomed its first patients, beginning with people on the autistic spectrum, then working with addiction before broadening to a full mental health service organisation. We now do lots of work around eating disorders, trauma, generalised anxiety and depression. There is a huge range of patients here, both adults and younger people. Equine-based therapy has become more and more accepted over the last few years; we get referrals from the NHS, hospitals and local government bodies, and we are continuing to work hard to build a solid evidence base that proves it not only works but it works fast – in many cases, a lot faster than in clinical environments.'

Most horse-loving people will swear by a horse's intelligence and empathy, but the data gathered by Dr Liefooghe and other clinicians meant these claims were starting to be quantified more scientifically. Dr Liefooghe published a book in 2019, *Equine-Assisted Psychotherapy and Coaching*, using carefully gathered evidence to reinforce how powerful horses can be in a therapeutic setting. 'I wrote a whole chapter about how anthropocentric our world view is,' he explained. 'We start from our own human perspective and go from there. And in doing so, we also anthropomorphise horses rather than seeing them for what they really are – creatures from whom we can learn a huge amount. One example of this is how incredible they are at looking after themselves. They will never stay in a place that feels unsafe for them, whereas we as humans hang around far too long. Sometimes we even look for more trouble in our lives, because, too often, we don't know what's good for us.

'Horses are also excellent at emotional regulation, and can teach us so much in that field,' Dr Liefooghe added. 'If a horse and rider are out hacking, and there's a white bag flapping in the wind, the horse will spook. But 10 seconds later, the bag is gone, the horse has moved on, and its emotions are reset. As humans, we wake up in a certain mood and are almost doggedly determined to stick to that mood, committing to our misery. Horses can teach us that we don't have to do that. We can say, bang! I'm done with that, it's gone. On to the next thing. When we stop seeing ourselves as the centre of the universe, and only one particle in this interconnected solar system, we can learn a huge amount, but people can't always do that. Therapy helps people begin to see things from a different point of view; to step back and observe. To lie flat on your back and feel the dampness of the grass and the sun, and the horses walking around you. It grounds you, and makes you feel part of something, so that whatever you're thinking or feeling is not as consequential as you might believe.'

In her 2017 book *Tamed*, anthropologist and presenter Alice Roberts explains how scientific studies are beginning to elucidate how complex animal behaviour is, particularly in horses. Research shows that horses make facial expressions and recognise emotions in another horse's face. Another study showed that when horses are shown images of men making angry, frowning or happy faces, their heart rates responded accordingly, increasing when they sensed negative emotions and slowing down when they see a happy face. Their ability to communicate with us through language, such as pointing their head at feed buckets when handlers come closer, indicating they would like a snack, suggests that, while they are not born with the ability to speak our 'language', they are predisposed to learn it – even if it is still expressed non-verbally.

We seem to have only scratched the surface of horses' mental and emotional capabilities, which means there is still so much untapped potential in our relationship with them. But if the future of equestrianism is leading us down these paths of health, wellbeing, recreation and sport, several issues around accessibility need exploring. The positive side of equestrianism is that, compared to other sports, there are fewer barriers to entry in terms of gender and age. In terms of participation, equestrian sports are one of the only few where the majority of competitors are female. As a result, becoming a parent is less likely to disrupt competitors' careers, as maternity leave is more normalised and encouraged. There is also no gender specification between athletes and no requirement to identify as male or female to qualify, enabling men, women and members of the non-binary community to compete against each other on a level playing field, with equal prize money and access to all competitions. It is also more accessible and inclusive for transgender athletes, who are too often required to overcome various obstacles when entering into other competitive sports. Studies have also identified lower levels of homophobia among the equestrian community, with several high-profile athletes who are openly gay.

In terms of age, equestrianism is a hobby and sport that anyone can be involved with, no matter their date of birth. Riders' ages range from tiny toddlers to those in their eighties, nineties and beyond. Nobody embodied this more than Queen Elizabeth II, a lifelong horse-lover and breeder who, even in her nineties, was still seen riding through the grounds of her estates. Equestrian sports have several top-level athletes competing across a wide age range, including Nick Skelton, who won gold in the Rio Olympics at the age of 58. Elsewhere, Ian 'Captain Canada' Millar broke the record for the most Olympic appearances by any athlete, in any sport, when he show-jumped in his tenth Games in London, age 65. The eighty-eight-year-old Japanese Olympic dressage veteran Hiroshi Hoketsu was actively bidding (although ultimately unsuccessful) for a place on the 2020 Tokyo team. And the Australian Olympic delegation to Tokyo included 66-year-old grandmother-of-four Mary Hanna, the oldest athlete at the games, and 62-year-old Andrew Hoy, who won individual eventing bronze.

Today, the main barriers to horse riding fall into three categories: financial cost, accessibility, and lack of diversity. The first will be familiar to anyone who has longed for a horse of their own or to have the clothes, equipment and other paraphernalia that come with equestrianism, or even just the chance to enjoy regular riding lessons. I grew up in that pocket of privilege where I knew plenty of people who rode horses, but we couldn't afford regular lessons for long periods, let alone dream of ever having a horse of my own. As a child, I remember envying those who went to 'Pony Club' at weekends or had a horse to tend to after school. Still, looking back now, I can see how even being around horses was a privilege and one I was fortunate to experience at all. The issue with horse riding, as opposed to other extra-curricular activities like football or music, is the combination of different costs that gradually pile up. A thrifty teenager might earn lessons or free rides if they help out on a local livery each week, but most people are required to pay for riding lessons of their own. In the south of England, where I live, private lessons can reach up to £75 per hour and even a group lesson can be as much as £50.

On top of that, riders need suitable clothing, including a safety helmet that should, technically, be replaced every time it suffers a heavy impact. If a rider wants to pursue equestrianism on their own horse or even loan or part-loan a horse from someone else, the animal alone can cost thousands of pounds, depending on their age, health, breed and experience. Then there's stabling and grazing; feed, hay, water and bedding; vet bills and insurance; the saddle, tack and other riding equipment; and farrier, dentist and physiotherapy fees. Compared with a pair of football boots, or even ballet lessons or a new violin that are also too expensive for most, it's easy to see how those from lower income backgrounds, particularly children and young adults who are not yet financially independent, simply cannot afford the same access to horse riding as others.

Like with many physical hobbies and sports, accessibility can be another obstacle that prevents people from horse riding – although according to British Equestrian, the National Governing Body for horse sports in the UK, equestrian sport has a strong record in participation from people with disabilities. The Riding for the Disabled Association (RDA) currently works with 27,000 adults and children with disabilities across 500 centres around the UK, providing riding, therapy, fitness, skills development and opportunities for achievement and welcoming clients from a wide range of physical and learning disabilities, including autism. British Equestrian also invests in its Accessibility Mark programme, which aims to support commercial riding centres to ensure they have the confidence and ability to provide for riders with disabilities. There are also many role models in the equestrian industry; Great Britain's para dressage team, for example, remains undefeated at the Paralympic Games. The work carried out to help make riding more accessible to all has been incredibly positive, with consistently strong improvement in participants' communication, confidence, physical abilities and relationship-building. But there is more work to do, particularly in the aftermath of the COVID-19 pandemic when every RDA centre was forced to close for the first time in its 51-year history; at the time of writing, participant numbers had not yet returned to their pre-Covid levels.

The final big hurdle for equestrians to overcome is the lack of diversity in the industry. At 24 years old, British-Jamaican event rider Lydia Heywood has seen firsthand how important diversity is for encouraging others to try horse riding. Lydia began her equestrian journey aged 11 after her mum Claire suggested she give it a go at a local riding school on Saturday mornings. 'I don't do things by halves, though!' Lydia told me. 'As soon as I started, I desperately wanted us to have our own pony, so we got our first Welsh pony, Bella. She had a kind nature and was great for hacking out and learning the basics with friends around the yard, but she had no desire to be competitive, so around eight months later, our second pony River came into our lives. She was more of a feisty Ferrari – which is how I discovered my bravery and love of competing!'

Lydia began representing Jamaica at eventing in 2017, an achievement she knew would inspire others to venture into a sport where racial diversity is not typically high. She was invited to become a mentor at the Ebony Horse Club in Brixton. This riding centre makes horses and riding more accessible for young people in inner-city London. They teach riders from south London's most disadvantaged communities, helping them to build their confidence and learn new skills by providing opportunities through equestrianism. It's a particularly vital resource for young riders, as many of them rarely leave the city, and 96 per cent of riding centres nationwide are located in rural areas with lower than average ethnic diversity. When Lydia joined them as a mentor, she found they were both delighted and taken aback that she represented Jamaica, a nation many of the riders felt connected to through their cultural heritage. She began to think about how she could take her mentorship further: 'How can we forge a path for these talented riders to join me?' she asked. 'Diversity is lacking enormously and time is of the essence for young riders. I didn't have all the answers, but I wanted to do something – so I founded Cool Ridings!'

The Cool Ridings project uplifts and advocates for riders from all backgrounds and recognises that equestrian sport requires disposable income. Through her contacts and experience in the industry, Lydia has created a warm and welcoming community for riders around the UK and beyond, with the ultimate goal of realising 'podium potential' and leaving a legacy that changes lives for the better. 'Celebrating and supporting riders who can represent developing nations is powerful,' believes Lydia. 'Equestrian sport must move with the times to stay relevant and find new sponsors that competition prize funds and event organisers can benefit from. I'm delighted that, through

Cool Ridings and other initiatives, brands and magazines have been enthusiastic about standing with us to shine a light on new talent. It truly gives us a sense of belonging that we have not had before.

'Children can't be what they don't see. It is not a given that eventing will keep its slot at the Olympic Games, because the International Olympic Committee states that some of the most important values in the Games are safety and relevance to young people. I barely watched equestrian sport before the age of 20, which might seem peculiar as a fiercely competitive young rider. But the subconscious reason for that was the fact that it didn't have a global feel, as there were only a handful of nations being represented at the most elite levels of the sport. Celebrating diverse talent will encourage riders to pursue an equestrian career and allow our sport to start resembling the real world we all live in together.'

Lydia's passion for equality has inspired countless young riders from all backgrounds, including eventer, showjumper and Cool Ridings member 14-year-old Rupert Hyde. With mixed British and Nigerian heritage, Rupert spent much of his early life in Spain, where his love of horses was shared and nurtured by his mother. When they returned to the UK, they brought their family of Andalusian horses, also known as *Pura Raza Española*, one of which, a youngster known as Guapa Alhaurino, is now ridden by Rupert. He had been taking lessons since attending a bilingual school in Malaga, but it wasn't until he won a rugby and riding scholarship to Millfield School in Somerset that his love for competitive riding started kicking in. He now produces the ponies and horses he competes with and loves learning to connect with them. 'There are pros and cons to teaching a horse how to compete,' he explained. 'You have to be stoic enough to accept when things go wrong and come to terms with it being a lack of experience or something else altogether. But the pride you feel when it goes right surpasses all of that. There is a lot to take on board, but the satisfaction of success, or even just improving on a previous performance, leaves you with a good feeling at the end of the day. Sometimes you could kick yourself for your mistakes, but each round always teaches you something!'

The lack of diversity in riding doesn't seem to be holding Rupert back, a four times national finalist with an incredibly bright future and dreams of riding for Team GB in the Olympics, but he still recognises the imbalances within the industry and why diversity is so crucial. 'It shouldn't have to be important, but it is,' he said. 'And it will continue to be until the balances can be redressed. As a mixed-race rider, I have both white and black heritage, so I see two sides of the same world from two different perspectives. But the door has to open further to people of colour so that people who wouldn't normally think to ride horses are encouraged to do so. Think of how much talent we must be missing!' I asked Rupert about his role models and he told me he had huge respect for Lewis Hamilton: 'His commitment to his sport, along with his family's support, has been huge. Now he pushes through the best and worst aspects of sporting life to represent what matters and proves that success can happen to anyone with support and commitment. I also admire Lydia Heywood within the eventing world as she has taken on similar battles with countless obstacles in her way, but with less of the limelight that Formula 1 seems to attract. I wonder why we can't promote equestrian sports to mainstream audiences more?'

Everyone should be free to experience the joy of riding. Horses are part of our heritage and, like the people of the British Isles, Europe and the rest of the world, their beauty lies in the melting pot of history, geography and genetics that make them the animals they are today. When we see a horse grazing in the hills and dales of the British landscape, few of us wonder whether they evolved here or not, whether they count as 'native', or if they come from an esteemed breeding stud. Most of us see only an animal at peace, their lives interwoven with the landscape around them – just as humans evolve, travel, ebb and flow, and find a home wherever they are welcomed.

U

Who else but the horse can reflect both the tamed and untamed elements of our world, bound together in one warm, mortal body? To spend time with a horse is to peer into a mirror and into our own souls; they remind us of our own liminal existence, part way between the wild and the domesticated. We believe ourselves to be civilised, regulated, sensible, and yet everything we do is driven by the same primal urges that have guided us through the entire existence of our species. Beneath all the bravado, we simply want to eat, drink, sleep safely, belong to a community and reproduce – all simple behaviours that we have somehow overcomplicated. When we speak to and share spaces with horses, we are reminded of those simple needs, and the façade of what we *think* we might need melts away. Peace, good food, a healthy body and a herd of friends and lovers – what more could anyone wish for?

Throughout history, humans have valued horses for their strength, speed and temperament. Pulling chariots, milling apples, carting granite, carrying knights, hauling machine guns, shaping roads, felling trees and creating new Edens; there are few challenges we have set for horses to which they have not risen, even in the face of an increasingly mechanised and digitalised age. But we have also formed a unique bond with horses that, for the most part, we do not share with other animals. Just as Sleipnir slipped between worlds, horses have become our go-between, the link that binds our rigid human society to the wild creatures and spaces that exist outside, beneath sunshine, starlight and wide, open skies. Cattle are as strong as horses, but we do not love them in the same way; dogs can be as companionable as horses, but we infantilise the former while revering the latter. Neither cuddly pets nor expendable livestock, what is it about these extraordinary animals that ignites our curiosity and awakens our deepest, wildest selves?

In 1942, halfway through the Second World War, the Irish artist and author Robert Gibbings published *Coming Down the Wye*, a travelogue documenting his journey from the source of the Wye in the Cambrian mountains, down the Wye valley through several towns and villages, and discussing the history, folklore and wildlife he encounters, as well as conversations with the natives. His wife and two children had been evacuated to Canada two years before. Gibbings had settled into the life of a semi-bachelor, spending many long hours outside with just a notebook, sketchpad and microscope, always drawn to the rivers and streams that wove gently past him. His writing is as soft and sparkling as the water that flows through it, but his engravings also helped make his books popular. Trained as an artist in London, he became one of the founding members of the Society of Wood Engravers and was a major influence in the revival of wood engraving in the twentieth century. He loved the 'possibilities of expression' that engraving opened up: 'I began to enjoy the crisp purr of the graver as it furrowed the polished surface ... Clear, precise statement, that was what it amounted to. Near enough wouldn't do: it had to be just right.'

Close to the end of *Coming Down the Wye*, one of the chapters finishes with a small engraving, no larger than a business card in my own ancient copy. It shows a simple black pony with her head dipped down to drink, her body soft and relaxed, her coat glossy, and clusters of river grass reflected in the glassy water. The pony's name was Betty, and in his own words, Gibbings had acquired her to ride, stand still when he wanted to watch a bird and mind her steps through rough terrain. A pony, his friend observed, that would save him from walking and not keep him running. The same friend brought him Betty, and a saddle and bridle, and for the first time in the book, he begins to travel in the company of another creature. She is no majestic stallion, champion racehorse or pedigree mare; only a small, black pony at home in the Welsh hills, willing to share her life with a new companion. In those last short chapters, he rides Betty along the banks of the Wye until he comes to his final stopping place: the Blue Bell pub. After an evening of singing and drinking, he steps out into the night air and finds Betty outside where he had tied her up, obedient but restive and ready to carry him home. He mounts, moves forward and turns in the saddle for one last look at the silver river winding through the valley before turning back with Betty to wander over the hill and across the moor, riding home together under a black, starlit sky.

No matter how strange the future looks, how changeable and chaotic and unfamiliar our world has always been, our connection with horses continues to root us in the collective human experience. 'I love the sight and sound and smell and feel of a horse,' wrote the author C. S. Lewis, 'I'd sooner have a nice, thickset, steady-going cob that knew me and that I knew how to ride than all the cars and private planes in the world.' Those soft-souled, warm-blooded companions have shaped the landscape of Britain and beyond and shown us the best and worst of what our species can be. And still they remain our friends and helpers, carrying us away from a disappearing past and forward into an uncertain future. They are our beacons in the dark, connecting us through the mountainous centuries like fires in the night – because the way it feels to ride a horse now is the same as it has ever been. A feeling of freedom, exhilaration, power, comfort and friendship. Even in the face of all the unknown that lies ahead, to know the value of a horse is to hold fast to the beauty of life; to see our complicated world for the strange, magical place that it is, and to love every single living thing with whom we have the privilege of sharing it.

Acknowledgements

First of all, thank you to all the horses who have ever walked the Earth and all the ones to come. It has been a joy to get to know you better.

Thank you also to everyone who kindly offered to me their wisdom, expertise and passion for horses, particularly Will Steel at the British Horse Society, Tara Russell at Marwell Zoo, Brigitta Falcini at the Riding for the Disabled Association, Liam Bartlett at Warwick Castle, Dee Dee Chainey, Yarrow Townsend, Andy Robinson at the Weald & Downland Museum, the Kelly Mine volunteers, Ruth Chamberlain, Yaheya Pasha, Dr Andreas Liefooghe, Lydia Heywood, Rupert Hyde, Damian Le Bas and Raine Geoghagen, who allowed me to reproduce her poems 'Kushti Grai' and 'Koring Chiriclo II – a triolet'. A special thank you to Rina Quinlan for the beautiful tour of Knepp and for being such a kindred spirit. To Tom Cox for giving me my copy of *Coming Down the Wye*, and to Derek, Wendy and all my friends at the yard where Olive and I have been able to ride such lovely horses in the last few years – none more so than Roxy.

Big love to my editor Julie for always being wonderful, and to all my friends and family for supporting everything I do, particularly my mum Debbie who first introduced me to horses, and my mother-in-law Chris who continues to facilitate my love for them now! To my sisters Chloë, Hollie, Christie and Jenny for always taking a wholehearted interest in my writing, and to Mark Ranger and Imogen Wood for the constant creative support and friendship. Thank you to my dogs Pablo and Tequila, who are very important, and to my husband Dave, who is kind, handsome and selfless. Most of all, thank you to my little baby Olive, who makes every moment of every day more beautiful than the last.

Further Reading

Armitage, Simon. 2009. *Sir Gawain and the Green Knight*. London: Faber.

Chainey, Dee Dee. 2018. *A Treasury of British Folklore: Maypoles, Mandrakes and Mistletoe*. London: National Trust.

Defoe, Daniel. 1978. *Tour Through the Whole Island of Great Britain*. London: Penguin.

Dixie, Lady Florence. 1892. *Gloriana: Or, the Revolution of 1900*. London: Henry & Co.

Duke Cavendish, William A. 2012. *A General System of Horsemanship*. London: Trafalgar Square Books.

Frampton, George. 2018. *Discordant Comicals: The Hooden Horse of East Kent*. Kent: Ozaru.

Horwood, William. 1980. *Duncton Wood*. London: McGraw Hill.

Juniper, Tony. 2013. *What Has Nature Ever Done For Us?: How Money Really Does Grow On Trees*. London: Profile.

Liefooghe, Andreas. 2019. *Equine-Assisted Psychotherapy and Coaching: An Evidence-Based Framework*. Oxford: Routledge.

Lord Tennyson, Alfred. 9 Dec 1854. 'The Charge of the Light Brigade'. London: *The Examiner*.

Macfarlane, Robert. 2013. *The Old Ways: A Journey on Foot*. London: Penguin.

Monbiot, George. 2013. *Feral: Rewilding the Land, Sea and Human Life*. London: Penguin.

Morpurgo, Michael. 2017. *War Horse*. London: Egmont.

Ogilvie, Will H. 1922. 'The Hoofs of the Horses' in *Galloping Shoes*. London: Constable & Company Ltd.

Rackham, Oliver. 1998. *The History of the Countryside*. London: Phoenix.

Tree, Isabella. 2018. *Wilding*. London: Picador.

Vera, F. W. M. 2000. *Grazing Ecology and Forest History*. Oxford: CABI Publishing.

Warwick, Hugh. 2018. *Linescapes: Remapping and Reconnecting Britain's Fragmented Wildlife*. London: Vintage.

Webb, Mary. 1992. *Gone to Earth*. London: Virago.

References

Ainsworth, William H. 1834. *Rookwood*. London: Richard Bentley.

Bird, Isabella. 2003. *The Englishwoman in America*. Carlisle, MA: Applewood Books.

Bird, Isabella. 2017. *A Lady's Life in the Rocky Mountains*. 2nd edn. Oxford: John Beaufoy Publishing Ltd.

Carson, Rachel. 2000. *Silent Spring*. London: Penguin.

Chambers, David. 2021. 'Custard Creams and the CIA.' *The Blindboy Podcast*.

Chappell, Henry. 2015. *The Day, and Other Poems*. New York: The Scholar's Choice.

Church, Andrew, Becky Taylor, Neil Maxwell, Olivia Gibson and Rosie Twomey. 2010. 'The health benefits of horse riding in the UK.' University of Brighton: http://www.bhs.org.uk/enjoy-riding/health-benefits.

Cobbett, William. 2001. *Rural Rides*. London: Penguin.

Dennison, Walter T. 1891. 'Orkney Folklore: Sea Myths.' *The Scottish Antiquary, or, Northern Notes and Queries*. 5:19. 130–33.

Dickens, Charles. 1995. *Nicholas Nickleby*. Ware: Wordsworth.

Fiennes, Celia. 2009. *Through England on a Side Saddle in the Time of William and Mary*. London: Penguin.

General Seely, Jack. 1941. 'My Horse Warrior: Death of a Well-known Charger.' *The Times*. 5 April.

Geoghegan, Raine. 2018. *Apple Water: Povel Panni*. Clevedon: Hedgehog Press.

Geoghegan, Raine. 2019. *They Lit Fires: Lenti Hatch o Yog*. Clevedon: Hedgehog Press.

Gibbings, Robert. 1942. *Coming Down the Wye*. London: J. M. Dent & Sons.

Green, Charles W. 1965. 'A Romano-Celtic Temple at Bourton Grounds, Buckingham.' *Records of Buckinghamshire*. 17:5. 356–66.

Hardy, Thomas. 2005. *The Woodlanders*. Oxford: OUP.

Hayes, Alice M. 1910. *A Practical Guide to Side-Saddle Riding and Hunting*. London: Hurst and Blackett.

Hughes, Thomas. 1859. *The Scouring of the White Horse*. Boston: Ticknor and Fields.

Kolbert, Elizabeth. 2014. *The Sixth Extinction: An Unnatural History*. London: Bloomsbury.

Lady Dixie, Florence. 1881. *Across Patagonia*. New York: R. Worthington.

Lady Dixie, Florence. 1905. *The Horrors of Sport*. London: A. C. Fifield.

Lear, Linda. 2008. *Beatrix Potter: The Extraordinary Life of a Victorian Genius*. London: Penguin.

Le Bas, Damian. 2019. *The Stopping Places: A Journey Through Gypsy Britain*. London: Vintage.

Liefooghe, Andreas. 2019. *Equine-Assisted Psychotherapy and Coaching: An Evidence-Based Framework*. Oxford: Routledge.

Little Dot Studios. 17 June 2019. 'The Abandoned Camelot Theme Park: Drones in Forbidden Zones.' TRACKS (via YouTube).

McRae, Andrew. 2009. *Literature and Domestic Travel in Early Modern England*. Cambridge: Cambridge University Press.

North, Marianne. 2016. *Recollections of a Happy Life*. Australia: Leopold Press.

Noyes, Alfred. 2013. *The Highwayman*. Oxford: OUP.

O'Connor, Terry and Naomi Sykes. 2010. *Extinctions and Invasions: A Social History of British Fauna*. Oxford: Windgather Press.

Ottman, Jill. 2015. 'A Woman Never Looks Better than on Horseback.' *Persuasions Online*. 36:1.

Porter, Valerie. 1996. *Tales of the Old Woodlanders*. Exeter: David & Charles.

Rackham, Oliver. 1998. *The History of the Countryside*. London: Phoenix.

Roberts, Alice. 2017. *Tamed: Ten Species That Changed Our World*. London: Penguin.

Ryall, Anka. 2008. 'The World According to Marianne North, a Nineteenth-Century Female Linnaean.' *TijdSdhrift voor Skandinvristiek*. 29:1–2. 195–218.

Šandlová, Kateřina, Martina Komárková and Francisco Ceacero. 2020. 'Daddy, Daddy Cool: Stallion–foal relationships in a socially-natural herd of Exmoor ponies.' *Animal Cognition*. 23:3. 781–93.

Sewell, Anna. 2019. *Black Beauty*. London: Puffin.

Shteir, Ann B. 1996. *Cultivating Women, Cultivating Science: Flora's Daughters and Botany in England, 1760–1860*. Baltimore: Johns Hopkins University Press.

Shteir, Ann B. 1997. 'Gender and "Modern" Botany in Victorian England.' *Osiris*. 12:1. 29–38.

United Nations Convention to Combat Desertification. 2017. *The Global Land Outlook*. Bonn, Germany.

Watts, Dorothy. 1998. *Religion in Late Roman Britain*. London: Routledge.

Wells, H. G. 2012. *The Invisible Man*. London: Penguin.

Whittingham, Sarah. 2009. *The Victorian Fern Craze*. Oxford: Shire.

Xenophon. 2010. *On Horsemanship*. Whitefish, MT: Kessinger Publishing.

Index